What is being said about

Meet Me Under The Eiffel Tower

"…[The author's] honesty is refreshing and her experiences keep you turning the pages. This is a book to lay back and savor, since once started it is hard to put down….[T] is a story that will surprise and shock you but will keep you reading."

Judith Habert
San Diego Woman Magazine

"Meet Me Under The Eiffel Tower is a well written snapshot of time in the life of a divorced woman looking to regain her balance in life. It is a great reading escape to be paired with a glass of fine wine and a fireplace!"

Vince Meehan
Mission Valley News

Meet Me Under
The Eiffel Tower

Tasha Donahue

Copyright 2012 by Tasha Donahue. All rights reserved.

Names have been changed to protect the guilty.

ISBN 978 147 757734-9

With my sincere thanks to my editor, Robert Goodman, Silvercat, for his encouragement and support. I could not have done it without him. Merci beaucoup, Bob!

For information and comments:

UnderTheEiffelTower@gmail.com

Cover photography by Tasha Donahue

This is dedicated to all the women who need a little encouragement to be all they can be until kingdom come. Live life fully. Strive to thrive. Say yes to N.O.!

— td

Readers' Discussion Guidelines

Name what you think is the primary reason for the author's having written this book.

Describe a pivotal moment in her journey.

Do you see some of yourself in author's thinking and actions? What, for instance?

Do you think it is unlikely that a woman in her sixties would allow a lover half her age into her life?

Did the discussion of Nitric Oxide surprise you? What is your N.O. level right now?

According to this book, what is the one main thing in life we should strive for?

This author lists negative pleasure such as drugs, alcohol, gossiping or self-destructive tendencies. When you are faced with someone who gossips how do you handle the situation? (pg 16)

Do you agree with the author that only you are in charge of your own happiness? (pg 17)

The author mentions spiritual orgasm. Other than sexual have you experienced a *spiritual* orgasm? (pg 20,23)

Does love conquer all?

"Nurturing" a sense of closeness with one other person is one of the components for living a quality life. What are other components?

The author's personality reflects what astrological sign? Does that explain her personality? How does this sign reflect in her attitude, her risks, her lifestyle?

The author shares candidly many sexual experiences in her life. Does that mask her life "issues" which she only alludes to? Would you have preferred her to discuss them or are you happy with the funky tempo of her book?

Do you think her openness adds to the believability of the storyline?

Did you ever want to run away from home? If so, where did you go and what did you do to get yourself back on track?

What can you do to implement the lessons of this book?

Some Favorite Quotes

While we have the gift of life, it seems to me the only tragedy is to allow part of us to die whether it is our spirit, our creativity or our glorious uniqueness.   Gilda Radner

Life is not measured by the number of breaths we take but by the moments that take our breath away.   Unknown

It isn't until you come to a spiritual understanding of who you are – not necessarily a religious feeling, but deep down, the spirit within – that you can begin to take control.
Oprah Winfrey

Can you imagine a world without men? No crime and lots of happy, fat women.   Marion Smith and Nicole Hollander

Your time is limited, so don't waste it living someone else's life. Don't be trapped by dogma — which is living with the results of other people's thinking. *Don't let the noise of others' opinions drown out your own inner voice.* And most important, have the courage to follow your heart and intuition.   Steve Jobs

...just being ourselves is the biggest fear of humans. We have learned to live our lives trying to satisfy other people's demands.....Don't take anything personally. Nothing others do is because of you. What others say and do is a projection of their own reality, their own dream. When you are immune to the opinions and actions of others, you won't be a victim of needless suffering.   Don Miguel Ruiz

When you're always trying to conform to the norm, you lose your uniqueness, which can be the foundation for your greatness.
Dale Archer

A word to my readers: Segments of this book contain adult-oriented scenarios. So, my ami, if you are up to it, grab a glass of vin and take the journey with me. Sante.

Td

PART ONE

One

I admit it. I was running away from home. What better place than to Paris? OK, OK, I am not exactly seventeen. As a matter of fact, I haven't seen that number for decades but if you gauge age by youthful enthusiasm then I am young. I also don't look like Whistler's mother, which helps. I look and act younger than I am; it confuses the hell out of everyone. Such a problem!

It has been a hard couple years in California, for that matter all over the United States. The economy is still in the toilet; half of Americans are surviving with Prozac or endless prayers to Jesus or Mohammed. For me, I have just about had it with the endless parade of problems my grown children continually present. So, screw it. I decided to run away and find my zest for living once again, the very thing that once made me charming. This wasn't going to be easy as I hadn't enjoyed myself in a long time. All the burdens of life outweighed by far the moments of joy. I hadn't seen a ballet, listened to a concert, danced or enjoyed a museum in way too long. I hadn't dated for more than three years and then only briefly, and basically, well, basically, I wasn't happy. Pass the Prozac. I devoted myself to charities and church and walked the straight and narrow. Nearer My God To Thee? Then why was I unhappy? I'll tell you why. Companionship, adventure and love were missing. My spirit was dying. Prayer wasn't working. I was totally out of sync.

Why wasn't I dating? Eeegads, too long a story to go into. OK, then, I'll abbreviate it: I found my last "boyfriend" on R Tranquity.com. Everyone urged me that this was a more spiritual site than say, the ever-popular Catch.com. Eventually, Adolph shows up at my door. He actually flies in from Wyoming to meet me. He was an older man. Now for me to say he is "older" suggests he is really old. I am no spring chicken myself, remember. But he knew how to court a woman, I will say that for him. He had presence, something very rare these days. So what did I care about the slight age lie he told on R Tranquility's "spiritual" website? He was treating me well, for Pete's sake! How refreshing!

But, as we got to know each other, his story came out. He was obviously German. His father had worked for Hitler, for God's sake, and he was named to honor "the fuehrer". Holy crap. He was in Hitler's youth group but, in fairness, most of the boys were required to be in that boy scout-type organization. There was no choice back then. Hmmm. But the dates and his age didn't match up. How could he be sixty-five and been part of it all? He had to be seventy-five or eighty. In the end, I couldn't blame him for what his father did but I hated the over-bearing way that he dictated everything to me. And I hate lies. Just tell me the truth, for God's sake; I am likely to find out, anyway. Don't lie.

To make things even more infuriating it seemed "my" Adolph could maintain an erection better by *making love standing up*. Dear lord, I was expected to stand on one tippy-toed foot, wrap the other around him and hope it worked *for him*. It sure as hell did not work for me. After explaining to him that I was neither an Olympic gymnast nor a prima ballerina, crestfallen, he agreed to get us back into bed. Oh, yeah, he didn't like me to talk when he was making love to me. No talking allowed. Well, it would be easier to expect our planet to stop spinning on its axis. No talking? What did the dictator have in mind next: Withholding food and water? Back I went to R Tranquility.

Six months before Adolph, I had a very brief fling with someone I thought I could have a future with. You have to recognize that I am either naïve, stupid or the eternal optimist. Maybe all three. I am an Aries, after all. I tend to believe what someone tells me. When John, who in his earlier life served as a Secret Service agent for the Presidents of the United States and their families, proved to be a total liar and commitment-challenged. The relationship quickly dissolved.

Before John I hadn't dated for four years. I was involved with a man who I actually fell in love with (it has only happened twice in six decades). I had dated him for two plus years and reluctantly decided he was looking for a meal ticket. He was a walking financial disaster. Discouraging, isn't it? So I gave up on dating. Can you blame me? Still, the heart is a lonely hunter. I was depressed. I wanted, *needed*, to have some fun. I wanted a companion and friend. OK, maybe more.

So off I went.

I landed in Paris for three months on September first. Rehab from depression and celibacy. But don't get me wrong. I really did not go to Paris for sex. I went to fill my spirit with art, music, good food, and new friends. Whatever else happened was of little consequence. I was trying to break the pattern of my sluggish endorphins. My shrink told me I was heightening the "pleasures sensors" in my brain. You betcha! I had been to Paris seven times before. I already knew I liked it.

I was supposed to live there for a year almost a decade ago but then my youngest son, at the last moment, elected to have brain surgery. Really. That is the honest-to-God truth. I wouldn't lie about such a thing. My trip, of course, was cancelled and I stayed in California to be around just in case I was needed. And I was, of course. I love my children, don't get me wrong, but…well, life has a way of sucking you back into it and before you know it, you are a decade older, your portfolio is half what it should be and your dreams are lost and forgotten.

So where was I, anyway? Oh yeah, Paris: "The City of Lights", of art, of metro musicians, of cuisine, wine, scarves and the odd combination of fabulous cathedrals and cheating husbands….what's not to love (as long as those cheating SOBs aren't *your* husband)?

Before I even left, I had been on Paris Craig's List for months looking for an apartment. Gads, I had carpel tunnel syndrome from too much desktop typing. Anyway, I couldn't help but notice Paris Craig's List had a section for men and women. I don't like provocative ads blaring "Women Looking for Men"; my pride gets in the way. It seems a little cheesy, frankly, that a classy dame like me should lower herself to advertise. Still, I wanted to make friends so I put an ad under "Platonic" and history took its course. *However, ...*

There is no "platonic" in France.

I had met him before I even left California via email. On my second day in Paris we met under the Eiffel Tower. He turned around, smiled and called my name. Effortlessly, I returned the smile. This was going to be fun, I thought.

His name was Jules.

Two

I boldly declared to my sisters that this Paris trip and anything that might happen was to be my "Last Hurrah". They told me I was crazy. Honestly, I couldn't take American men any more. But, it was my duty, my responsibility, wasn't it, not to let Adolph be the last lover in my life? I didn't want to die thinking of *him*! You can understand that, can't you?

Jules, Jules, Jules. He was an unlikely candidate to be my next – and possibly – last lover. First, he was too young. I thought he was forty when I emailed my two sisters and asked if they thought forty was too young for a potential lover. I received two quick responses: "Go for it!" We have this new, modern and awful term called "cougar" but I have never actually been one who wanted to take up with young men. It was seedy. I always believed that we maximize our chances of a successful long-term relationship with someone closer to our own age. But, it is not necessary to marry every guy you have ever gone out with. That is the difference.

I never thought I would have anything in common with a younger man. Then I found out he was not forty; he was thirty! My daughter laughed and said: "Mom! We are in the same dating pool!" I laughed, too. My boyfriend was *younger* than hers! Look, this really wasn't a competition. It just happened Jules was younger than he looked. He had an old soul with a young body, which at the time appeared better than an old body with a young soul.

So, as I said, I met Jules under the Eiffel Tower. It doesn't get any more romantic than that. He was dressed in a conservative business suit, had very short hair, eyeglasses and looked exactly like the photo he had sent me. He said my name and reached out to shake my hand. No lightning bolts. No earthquakes, just a quiet, reserved personality. I thought I might have found a new, good French friend who could help me navigate the complexities of French culture and maybe help improve my fledgling, pathetic French. My thoughts never went beyond that. Believe me, I never lie; it is one of my biggest pet peeves.

In ten minutes we talked like old friends. It was an easy conversation. I liked that. We did what I call a "Walk 'n Talk", ended with a cup of coffee and agreed to meet again. We did. Jules was such a nice person with a thoughtful, gentle way about him. By our third meeting, I was looking forward more to seeing him. He quickly became my best friend in Paris. He was protective, a gentleman and lo and behold! *A great listener.* Can you believe that? I had never met a man who was a great listener. It was new to me. Revolutionary. This in itself is a tremendous thing for a man of any age but a miracle for a young man. He was gaining my attention.

By our fourth date I was attracted enough to be excited at seeing him. Because of his reserved nature, he didn't appear flirtatious, which allowed me to relax and enjoy the moment. But on our fourth date he took me home early from our touring that afternoon. I wondered why we came home so early, Maybe, I thought, he had to get back to work. Nope! Wrong again, I am happy to report. When we sat down on the couch, he took my hand and kissed it. This is a great way for a man to see how interested a woman is. It should be included in school curriculum: *How To Make Sure A Woman Wants To Be Kissed 101*. Kiss her hand and watch the reaction. It should be taught in singles seminars, on-line dating services, published in books and float from the skywriting planes above. A woman has the chance to pull away or smile, thus acknowledging her level of interest. Me? I smiled.

Then he kissed me on the mouth. Now, listen, it had been a long time since I was kissed. Granted, I was not sure about any of this, but, damn, it was nice to be kissed again! My lips hadn't turn to rust, after all. So, we indulged in a few more kisses and he easily slipped me over his lap facing him. Again, I was surprised but fought my usual bad habit of saying "no" like I had been for years. Where, however, was all this leading?

Hell, you know where this was leading! Still, I was confused. Did this young man actually want to start a relationship or was he looking for a quick roll in the hay? *And did it matter?*

He did not want a committed relationship. "I cannot give you what you want. I work long hours and you need to go out and have fun." Hmmm, I thought.

Puzzled, I pursued a line of questioning. "So", I wondered aloud "do you want to be... lovers?" I whispered it just in case God was listening.

"No. We cannot be lovers if we do not love each other…"

Huh? "Well, what is it you want then?"

He hesitated. Silence filled the air.

"Sex partners?" I whispered almost inaudibly, trying to help my new best French friend. I am a very helpful person.

He nodded.

Hmmm. Now that seemed decidedly *unromantic*. I was going to have to think about this. While I tried to escort him to the door, we once again became entangled in affectionate pursuits. His conservative personality apparently didn't transcend his sexual nature (thank God). He was all over me at the door and finally, I convinced him I would give this all some thought and pushed him out to the closet-size elevator in my building.

Emerson must have known with his quote "The ancestor to every action is a thought."

And, holy cow, did I give it more thought!

Three

OK, let's freeze that last proposition for a moment. What would give me pause to even *consider* Jules's offer? Where did I stand on sexual encounters versus morality? Could I balance my middle class Christian ethics with... with...well, with my "needs"? Then I remembered a few books I had read, one on the, admittedly scientific topic of Nitric Oxide. Now, don't cringe; this is a vital field of study; it is an important one to all women *and* their men but most especially older women.

While I wasn't in menopause when I met Jules, still the messages in Dr. Christiane Northrup's book, "The Secret Pleasures of Menopause" resonated with me. Basically, it encouraged saying yes to N.O. (Nitric Oxide). You heard me. Let that become the motto of our newly forming union, the AF-KNO (American Federation of Kissing and Nurturing Organization). "Yes to N.O." Maybe I am thinking too small; perhaps, it should be The International Federation of Kissing and Nurturing Organization...No, maybe I should think bigger: The Interplanetary Federation....OK, OK, maybe I am getting ahead of myself.

"Nitric Oxide" is the spark of life according to Northrup. It is not the laughing gas given at your dentist office. Nitric Oxide is one atom of nitrogen and one of oxygen and it determines physical, emotional, spiritual and sexual wellness. I call it the WOW Molecule. Unfortunately, we women over fifty usually don't have enough. No secret to most of us.

The more I read, the more I learned to respect this little atom. And guess what? Sexual pleasure is associated with the release of nitric oxide from the lining of your blood vessels. It helps blood flow to all vital organs. *Bless it!* Sufficient amounts of N.O. trigger positive emotions: happiness, joy, strength, and hope. It improves mood and feeds the spirit. It sort of validates what all those would-be lovers have been telling us women since we were teenagers: Sex is healthy. Sex is good for you (not that they really were concerned about our health while in hot pursuit of our bodies). But those "lines" they gave us now are backed up by researchers, scientists and doctors who concur. Who'd have figured? But N.O. levels can be elevated without sex, so don't kid your self on that account. I am not advocating we all navigate the hills and valleys of America or the world at large to donate our bodies to the scientific study of Nitric Oxide.

Still, the mind, body, soul connection cannot be ignored. *N.O. propels you to live a more positive, self-fulfilling lifestyle.* When you are happier you attract people and experiences that complement the positivity within you. *There is nothing more attractive than a happy, confident person.* We are drawn to happy people. I met this charming man at the Y in my area who, at age seventy-five, loved his job. He loved being with people, loved helping them to understand the resistance machinery and loved helping them achieve their goals. He laughed easily and smiled often. He drew everyone to him. He was a magnate. Clearly, he had a high degree of N.O.

N.O. turns on the production of special chemicals in your body (neuro transmitters). It carries messages from the brain to the nervous system. Pleasure increases the beta endorphins that improve mood and help you to deal with the problems in your life. N.O. helps process healing and boosts immunity. OK, OK. Let's not get too technical here. But, it *is* essential to becoming a better *balanced*, healthier person. And *balance is the goal*.

So how do we increase N.O. in our lives? Here goes (and you have heard this all before): *live healthier lifestyles, exercise, control weight, sufficient water* and *sleep* and (tada!) *an increase of pleasure*. Yippee! Even positive *thinking* immediately boosts our N.O. levels. There are seventy million women in the US over forty-five who need to look at that because as we go through menopause we often suffer a lowered N.O. level.

But, hey, don't get me wrong; pleasure comes in more forms than sex. If you have a partner, pleasure can come in dosages of cuddling, hugging, kissing, touching, shared humor, *listening* to and caring about each other. It can also come through massage, yoga, laughter, friendship, calming music, and anything that gives you *positive* pleasure. In Paris it was the music, the art, the opportunities for growth in all sectors of my life that raised my levels off the charts! Oui! Oui! Oui!

Be realistic, though; there is such a thing as *negative* pleasure, such as drugs, alcohol, gossiping, anything that ultimately is destructive or self-destructive. You are the captain of your ship. You write the book of your life. You and only you are in charge of your happiness. Associate only with positive people; they will hold you accountable. While Mae West might have been quoted: "Too much of a good thing can be wonderful", the truth is too much is still too much. *Any at all negative pleasure* neutralizes the quality of *positive* pleasure. So don't let this information lead you astray. Too much of a good thing *can* be wonderful but *responsibly define* "good thing". What I am saying is that *no man, child, sibling or partner can make you a happier person; only you can*. Once you are, you will be received and viewed differently, more attractively as a human.

According to Northrup your body is turned on and kept healthy by high levels of N.O. *It is the fountain of youth!* That is one fountain I want to take a long, cool drink out of. She reminds us that we were created in a last burst of energy of nitric oxide, your father's orgasm. *Thanks for the visual, Doc.* N.O. can help to heal your body, your life and in turn affect the lives of so many more. All pleasures saturate your body and brain in life-giving oxide. N.O. is the answer! N.O. is our mantra!

What is your guilty pleasure? Before you answer that I should tell you that is a trick question. Why does guilt have to be associated with pleasure? What would make anyone think that pleasure isn't related to our spiritual life? Yes *spiritual* life.

Some thinking belongs in another century, another place. At my church there was more than one strange reaction to my trip to Paris (not that I dare tell them about the men). One lady I knew, an elder (my age) of our church and a nice but very conservative woman asked after my return from Paris why she hadn't seen me for awhile.

"I've been to Paris for three months" I gushed.

"Oh," she looked at me "What did you do there?"

"I had fun!"

"Oh". Startled by my candor, she struggled to react, muted by my honesty.

"And I am going back for another three months!" I bragged (stupidly), enthusiastic still about my favorite subject: Paris.

She couldn't fathom the idea. She excused herself and went, allegedly, to look for someone. She just didn't know what to say or how to react to the very concept of pleasure.

In my women's spiritual book club I suggested that we study the topic of pleasure and its effects on us and its relationship to our spirituality. You could have heard a pin drop. Silence. They, too, were afraid to broach the subject of pleasure.

Pleasure seems to be associated with guilt, with something we should not dare to experience. It appears to have more tolerance by society if you are young. God forbid you should have sexual needs/pleasure after fifty! That normally is the thought process by young, immature critics who can't imagine Grandma and Grandpa needing each other in the middle of the night. Boy, oh boy, are they wrong! Many baby boomers will verify that sexual needs do last a lifetime.

Sexual pleasure certainly, even today in many countries, is not to be experienced by women. Only men in these countries are allowed to have sexual pleasure. But that, of course, is self-pleasure, therefore, *negative* pleasure. According to Northrup, *pleasure is really only positive if we share it in some way with the universe.* If our molecules, serotonins and endorphins are in balance, we are healthier and send out healthier messages to the world surrounding us. We, as better beings, reflect that on to the communities around us. It is our Personal Peace Plan for the world!

As far as spirituality goes there appears to be a link. I believe that I am a part of a larger, infinite body of Energy that I call God. Some call it your Higher Source, Mother God, Father God etc. Have you ever shed a tear during an intimate sexual encounter"? In the "The Heart and Soul of Sex" author and Ph.D. Gina Ogden, states "Sexual response is more than physical. It is a rich and complex experience that involves our whole beings. We are actually hard-wired to experience sex multi-dimensionally."

I think we are hard-wired to experience *pleasure* multi-dimensionally. Have you felt the pure joy of being connected with another individual in a special way? Have you been moved to tears by a musical aria, a touching movie, a courageous friend, a work of art, a stunning sunset, or a new baby?

I remember the birth of my first son. I was in a glass-enclosed birthing unit with my doctor and the attending nurse. Something magical, *spiritual* happened that day in that glass unit. Silence surrounded us as he was born, a healthy nine-pound boy. But now, thirty-seven years later, I can still remember an energy force that permeated that birthing room. It was what I then would have called an angelic presence witnessing the birth. It was profound and holy. It was cosmic and universal. It was God. It was overwhelming, multi-dimensional and real, and the intensity of those feelings that day so long ago has never been forgotten.

Remember in the movie "Julie and Julia" when Julia Child and her husband, Paul, arrived in France and were at a restaurant eating lunch? Julia was beside herself with the full dimensional experience of that divine fish and tried to share that joy with her husband. He took a bite and nodded his approval and went on with his lunch, unmoved by its perfection. Julia, however, was in ecstasy. Every nuance of the meal moved her to her soul. That certainly for her was a multi-dimensional experience. That deep awareness is what I am speaking of.

The energy that exists between you and another – in all its' many formulas - surely has a connection to the greatest source of Energy. When you feel profoundly moved in a sexual encounter (or whatever speaks intensely to your heart) it is my belief that you experience the divine. This happened repeatedly throughout my adventures in Paris: attending an opera, biking a winding path around Versailles or enjoying a fabulous ballet at Opera Garnier. I have experienced it here, at home. For instance, as I attended with a friend, the opera "Turandot" and listened breathlessly to the perfect finale aria. That spiritual connection to the Infinite washed over my body and soul strengthening it, enabling me to give more to my world. I was profoundly grateful for those moments. Northrup calls it a "spiritual orgasm"! Hallelujah.

But behind this knowledge and acceptance lies a moral fiber that cannot be ignored. We need to be able to be at peace with our decisions and not regret them. We need to honor God by honoring the persons we are.

So in what direction would this N.O. information lead me? Would I take Jules on or not? Would I, should I, say yes to N.O.?

Four

Every woman is different, of course. Why, how, when, where we decide to take a new lover is individual. But it had been a long time before I, how shall I put this delicately…jumped anyone's bones *(OK, so I am indelicate)*. More than three and half years, remember! The absence of sex can make for a very grumpy person. Ask my friends. Ask my *ex-friends*. Before those two failed attempts at "relationships" with Adolph and John, it had been four years since being with a man. I wasn't exactly prowling the bars, purring as I wend my way from one man to another. Far from it.

But if I were faithful to my Christian upbringing there would be no sex unless I was married. *Forget that*. The only time in my life that I *didn't* have sex was when I was married. I am a "reasonable" Christian, not an evangelist or a nun. Nor am I what might be termed "immoral"… somewhere in my own comfort zone between the two, closer I figure, to my Christian upbringing than it is sometimes convenient to be. Still, I figure, if God created me with a libido, with a need to give and receive affection then why should I deny that element of my persona… *forever just because I am single*? It insults the intelligence. As I stated, I was clearly used to saying "no" not "yes" to sex. The balance of needs, wants and morals is different for every woman; we become jugglers in the circus of our lives.

I remember visiting my sisters in Florida, sitting on the patio, drinking wine. One thing led to another and once again we were discussing the absence of men from our lives. Maybe you have had the same discussion. Out of the clear blue sky, my younger sister says: "How many lovers have you had; two hundred?" *Two friggin' hundred?!* Meow, meow. I wanted to punch her right in the nose but we were drinking good wine and I hadn't finished. Hell, why didn't she just call me a slut? OK, maybe she did. But I am no basketball player, after all. Of course, there are sisters and girlfriends we hold dear with whom we reveal everything but if *they* haven't had sex for decades any sexual conduct is going to seem well... shocking. I never took a vow of chastity, after all. Should I suffer because *they* were in denial of their sexuality and I wasn't? I don't think so. But trying to talk about sex with a woman who hasn't had any for decades is often an exercise in futility. She basically is in denial. Sad really.

We don't have to be past fifty to look back on life, at the losers we chose, the hilarious relationships we endured and the ones who got away. We continued on into the conversation, now counting, to the best of our disintegrating memory cells, just how many men we each had had in our lives. I was the only honest one, apparently, as they became lost in the idea of counting men they had long ago (and happily) forgotten. I came up with my total, which, believe me, was far below the projected number. They were just jealous, that's all, I reminded myself. I don't answer to them; I answer to myself.

This discussion wouldn't end itself. It led to our first boyfriends/lovers. I hadn't thought about him for decades: Brett was my first lover. When I was still a twenty-one year old virgin I met Brett, a senior at Northwestern University in Evanston, Illinois. He was a handsome, preppy guy, already accepted into Stanford Law School, allegedly with a bright future. His deceased father had left him six and half million bucks when he died and went to heaven.

Brett's mother was an upper crust San Franciscan who was so infuriated at his dating a mere "secretary" that she pulled some connections and got him drafted into the army right after college graduation. Off he shipped to Viet Nam. You might refer to her as the MFH – Mother From Hell. Anyway, Brett went to his own drummer, although he was a bit eccentric for a twenty-two year old. He liked to talk backwards and see who could understand him. It irritated me to no end. But I was really flexible in those days. That's youth. I was more interested in his body than his mind, anyway. I will give him the benefit of the doubt and assume he gave up that backward talking eccentricity somewhere along life's path.

I can actually remember the date of My Great Decision: August 11, 1967, my sister's birthday. I can remember thinking I was tired of saying no (That kind of thinking always gets me in trouble). This was the middle of the sexual revolution and the bus was leaving me far behind. So I unabashedly lured in Brett with the obvious: I was ready for him. Can't say he protested. But there were no long drum rolls, no showers of confetti, no lightning striking my heart or regions there below. In fact, I was rather sore.

Fortunately, I am tenacious. Brett must have appreciated that at the time and we did not give up. For many, even those with a curious sexuality and strong libido, sex is an acquired taste (so to speak) rather similar to caviar. One gets to know the good stuff from the bad stuff only if one tries enough of the "stuff" out. I never learned to appreciate really good sex with Brett but I am sure he loved my eager-bunny libido and natural sensual nature. I can remember him saying: "You are the most inherently passionate woman I have ever met". Even though that comment came from a mere twenty-two year old (what the hell did he know, after all, at twenty two?), he, God bless him, wasn't far off track.

I don't know what happened to Brett. He visited me once in uniform and then took off for Viet Nam. He may have rolled that six and half mil into a billion buckaroos by now. He may also have lost most of it in market swings and be penniless. Or his dear, young bones might be buried deep in Viet Nam somewhere. But I still remember him and smile when I think of him. That is more than I can say about a lot of his successors.

But there was more to my life than my past...

Five

On the second day I spent with Jules, when I was not yet aware that it might turn into an intimate relationship, I spoke freely of another Frenchman, Pierre. I blogged about him and referred to myself as "The Motorcycle Princess". I also met Pierre through Craig's List. At my suggestion we met under the Eiffel Tower. I didn't know he drove a motorcycle. We both were eager for a "cultural exchange", a meeting in which he could better his English and I, my French. Seemed harmless enough and it was the same guise under which Jules and I met. Eventually, I would catch on to this "Cultural Exchange" idea. While there are actually those who do want a language exchange, most of the men used it as an opportunity to meet visitors and English-speaking women. My guess is they felt we might be more amenable to a brief fling than the wiser French women, who were already burnt out with their mischief. At the time, I did not really understand; I looked forward to these meetings to have someone show me Paris and help me navigate the culture.

I learned to ask these men in the first hour if they were married. Jules smiled broadly (with relief?) and quickly said "No". He would be the exception to the rule.

When Pierre walked me over to where he parked his motorcycle he was clearly expecting me to be very flexible with our transportation mode. I flinched. I don't like motorcycles. I think they are dangerous. Now what was I going to do? I quickly recovered and said "D'accord" (OK) and he put a huge helmet on my head, then his, and I asked a pedestrian to take our photo. My girlfriends, all grandmothers like me living conservative lives with their first and only husbands back home, would think this was hilarious. Me, I just thought at that moment it was risky. But, I was here "looking for adventure" as my blog stated. I couldn't back down on adventure when it presented itself, could I? If I died this day, I would leave a nice insurance policy to my son. That was a comforting thought. See how practical I am?

Off we jolted straight into the traffic along the Seine. The traffic: now that is a subject unto itself. Paris traffic was never-ending. It came from all directions feeding from suburbs, businesses, tourist buses, cars, taxis and, yep, motorcycles. Masses of 'em. Those cyclists weaved in and out of traffic without signaling, passing irreverently by the cars who could not navigate so easily. Smaller, faster motorcycles carried smug, confident drivers who knew they would get to their goal before the cars. It was all one big macho display. So French.

I closed my eyes. Zip, zap, zip. At first, I leaned into Pierre, wrapped myself around his leather jacket and held on tightly. It was a gorgeous, sunny day in Paris and he appeared to know how to drive safely. Eventually, I relaxed, straightened up, smiled to myself, thrilled with seeing the city this way. He would yell back at me as he whisked me through the rues of Paris what building this or that was. Most of the time, I couldn't hear his words, thick with French accent, as they flew off with the wind. He plunged into the traffic pointing out the Pantheon, Ile St. Louis, St. Germaine-des-Pres and finally we stopped at the

Palais Royal for a Walk 'n Talk. I exhaled. This was fun and I was still breathing!

After I caught my breath I asked him the same question as I had Jules two days earlier:

"Are you married?"

This was not met with the broad smile given to me by Jules but rather a serious scoff:

"But, of course!" he mumbled, hurrying through the gardens trying to divert me from the subject. I was not going to let this go. I forged again into the topic.

"Does your wife know you are here with me?" I continued, stuck on the idea.

"No" he shrugged, "she does not. What she doesn't know won't hurt her…" Hmmm.

"How would you feel if she were with someone else now?" I interrogated him fearlessly.

"If I don't know, I don't care…" Pierre shrugged again and suggested we head over to a café for a bite to eat. After a leisurely lunch and easy conversation we headed home.

Zipping through the streets of Paris, wind in my face, I relaxed and released my death grip on Pierre. How strange, I thought are the cultural differences. He wasn't even going to try to hide his marital status from me. It was what it was. But what was it? Maybe, it was just a "cultural exchange" I reasoned to myself.

But Pierre spoke excellent English; I doubt I could improve it and so far we weren't attempting French verb conjugations….

He stopped up at my apartment for a few brief moments to look at my French language notes.

"You don't need to learn French" he concluded. "Everyone speaks English here."

I didn't invite him to stay. Instead, I escorted him to the door. Truthfully, it had been a pleasant day, an experience of a lifetime and I had survived. Now it was time to say au revoir. I thought I was quite clever to lightly kiss him on each cheek as is the custom in France but he then looked confused. What, I thought, is he confused about?

"That's the way you say good-bye in Paris, isn't it?" I explained.

"No", he smiled slightly, "It is not. This is the way we do it in Paris". He lifted my face up to his, cupping my head in his hands and kissed me square on the mouth three times. Well, that answered my question about his idea of "cultural exchange".

"But…" I began to protest.

"No buts," he smiled and kissed me again before the opportunity passed.

Hmmm.

"What is it you want from me?" I asked quietly.

"Nothing… Everything" he corrected himself, grinning.

My, my. Those Frenchies are sure up front about everything, aren't they?

"I…I…I…don't know" I stammered. "I don't think I want more. You are married, after all. I don't think it would work for me."

"No problem. No obligation. Think about it and I will talk to you about another ride through Paris, either way".

Yikes! Was this going to happen every time I went out? Does anyone actually date before they jump into bed in Paris? Were all middle-aged women such easy marks? Maybe. Occasionally. Probably.

I had been in Paris less than a week.

I told Jules my story. He was quite interested. Remember this happened prior to his fourth date declaration of sexual interest. Oui, oui, he remembered he told me to go out with others, but his curiosity was apparent. He really was very sweet. He wanted to know everything. I didn't reveal much. Generally, it is not a good policy to talk about other men to the man you are with.

But there was more to my life than this…seriously!

Six

Menopause! Sooner or later the Monster pounds on our door staking its claim on all women (and inadvertently our men). The Big Monster: Menopause! It stalks us all and for many of us detonates like a classified atomic bomb. Surprise! The joys and challenges of womanhood present themselves once more. The Big Menopause Monster can change everything.

Just when we have gained life experience, just when we have gained confidence, just when we are at our physical and mental best, whamooo! The Big MM finds you! It is a rare woman, indeed, who is not drastically affected by it as is her partner.

I was forty-five when the Big MM seized control of my body and, I might add, in a not too subtle fashion. My husband, a doctor, kept telling me my body was reacting from the death of my father the year before. I was too young for menopause said he, dismissively, with a wave of his hand.

I knew he was wrong. I looked at him like he was the Village Idiot, shook my head, mumbled something nasty and then I went to the doctor. I had every damn symptom possible and I was in it from my head to my toes. But, he, genius that he was, thought he knew more about The Big MM than I did. Go figure.

A week after the appointment my husband remembered I had seen the doctor and asked me the outcome. "So how did that appointment go?"

"Like I expected" I responded, still a bit annoyed. "I am smack dab in the middle of menopause!"

"You're kidding?" he stupidly responded. Husbands are always stupid about menopause even if they are doctors. Who the hell would kid about The Big MM, anyway?

There was no warning for me, no irregular periods, nothing. I just stopped my periods cold turkey. I was having hot flashes morning, noon and night. Nocturnal were the worst. I could feel the waves of heat starting at my toes escalading up their way through my body to my head. Irritability, swift changes in mood were apparent to everyone, even me. Open the window, it is hot in here. Close the window. Open, close…I was exhausted and dragging, and well, it was not a pretty picture.

Even if we hadn't had marital problems already it surely would have taxed our relationship. I bet that if research were conducted they would find some link between mid-life menopausal women and divorce. I won't blame my divorce on menopause but menopause is an alert to the aging process, to life passing, to the chances left for happiness. It is a summons to stop and reflect where life is at and an opportunity to reassess where we want our life to head. It is a formal petition to do what needs to be done to ensure happiness the second half of our life. As you sweat in 40 degree weather it shouts: *We are all mortal!* Yep, when one goes head first into this demonic pool called menopause, one starts to reassess her time here on terra firma.

I wanted control of my body and my life back. For me an important part of the remedy came through exercise. I started walking, added biking and then swimming, one after the other. My butt actually lifted! Apparently, I reversed the gravitational forces of my butt! Damn, I was proud. Exercise helped to balance the serotonins in my brain, which clearly cried SOS. I started to look better and feel better. For the next eighteen years I stayed on that exercise kick, two hours a day six days a week. There is something about a woman who is on that track. She does become happier, calmer. She looks better and the glow that comes from that attracts people to her.

Yeah, you argue, I should find my peace within. I get that. I am aware and have worked on that for years. I have done due diligence to my spiritual life becoming a lifetime volunteer in a variety of charities and mission trips. I even started a spiritual group of women to discuss monthly a variety of important topics: ego, sacrifice, fear, forgiveness etc. But that is not what this book is about, is it? You can be multi-dimensional, can't you? You can if you dare. The recognition of multi-dimensionality is essential if we dare to live full lives on all levels of our persona. The spiritual connection to pleasure is what separates us from the animals.

I got off track. *How* does menopause effect women? There are loads of books out there and as we baby boomers experience this, the Big MM, more meaningful books are being written; we demand it.

Some women are forever changed by this initiation into Good Old Girls Club. Others bloom (*we hate those women, don't we?*). At the onset I was like a dog in heat. I needed sex badly, constantly and I didn't get anything because my husband and I weren't engaging in the sacred act for a very long time before I left him. *Makes for a grumpy woman*! Ask him; he would agree! That period of extreme neediness lasted about six months (It would have been a gift if I had had an active sex life with someone at the time).

Then: *Dum Da Dum Da:* A comatose state of that "special place" between my legs! Everything down there seemed to die! Morte. Finito. Gone. Depression followed which is easy enough to understand. Was I never going to have an orgasm again? Black shrouds covered my bed. Clouds lingered above my home. I sequestered myself away from the world. I became a recluse. Well almost.

I had decided to divorce before The Big MM but waited till three years later. I wanted to be sure my decision, after a long marriage, was not hasty or founded on emotions that were unreliable. So, in a way, I didn't mind – at first – loosing that libido. It was convenient. My husband and I never had to talk about it. Our no-sex union continued, unaffected.

Here's my beef: our pharmaceutical companies have done all this research to benefit men's drive and ability to have sex into infinity. Clearly, this is a male-driven research. There is very little, a minute amount really, of research done to benefit their partners: *women*. I have always been livid about that. Why encourage men and then not help their women? It makes no sense. So men get to have pleasure to the moment of death and women, well, women are just supposed to suck it up (no pun intended). We are not supposed to resent the idea that he will fully enjoy sex for decades in a way we are not able. Then, the merciful Grim Reaper claims you. No wonder we need chocolate!

I now belong to an HMO, Miser Permanente. A pox on their house! The first time I went to talk to the head of OB-GYN, he, about fifty-five years old, merely shrugged and suggested I grow old gracefully. *Grow old gracefully?* He is, of course, lucky I didn't, in my agitated condition, slit his throat!

Instead I replied, "Yeah, doc, sure. And if someone shrugged at you and told you not to worry about having orgasms any more, *how would you feel*? Would you be 'graceful'?"

"Maybe you should see our advocate for women..." he hastily scribbled in his notebook (probably noting my confrontational persona).

Recently, in an office visit to this female "advocate" she suggested that when the man was right for me "everything would be fine". I found this condescending and more than annoying and she knew it. *Does* love conquer all? I don't think so.

"It is *not* fine!" I snapped. "Men have tried to please me through these years after the divorce but, since menopause, this isn't happening for me. Give me some testosterone cream. Tell me what research is being done. Get me into a study group!" She, my age, remained unmoved. Apparently, we gals are just supposed to quietly, "gracefully" give up on this. Miser Permanente sure as hell didn't care.

Miser also won't do a saliva test. "We don't do that here". They pooh-poohed the idea and dismissed it as having been a bit weird. I went and had it done on my own buck to find out I had almost non-existent estrogen and testosterone levels. *Did that make me a neuter?* But my HMO will not look at that, either. I got a little wind of a *lecture* from my "advocate" about my being single and letting it (sex) all go. She had the audacity of bringing in a *morality* issue to me, aging woman that I was, worried about having an orgasm. *Morality?* It wasn't like I was bouncing from one relationship after relationship trying to get into the Guinness World Book of Records for Promiscuous Women. I hadn't had a sexual relationship at that time in years. She was buying into the male-dominated OB-GYN philosophy at Miser that encouraged women not to have sex; then there would be no problem. Right? I think she was a spy from my church where celibacy is expected if you are not married. OK, so a little paranoia slipped in…

But, here is my point: Kissing, touching, having sex with another human being is an important part of the *quality of life*. It is not the only part but for many of us, it is a big part. It balances the stings of life that come our way. We need these things, and I, even in my disabled stage, had no intention of giving that all up for lack of, of, of *resolution*.

Many women give up. They expect their husbands/lovers to understand and give up also. What a terrible expectation! It really is too much to ask. Then, all the nurturing tends to stop. Why get one party riled up when the other doesn't want sex? So the kissing and touching stops. The nurturing is lost. A couple becomes distant, platonic, more like a brother and sister, which may be acceptable, even a relief for some, but it sure doesn't work for everyone.

A couple of past lovers had no problems but most had multiple problems. So women are not the only one with issues. It takes two to tango. Men have their own set of sexual problems but let's not go there. Or, hell, maybe we should…

In the fifteen years since my divorce I have found men of all ages having endless ED issues. It is the most delicate thing you can talk to a man about. Most are in denial. Every excuse is presented: too tired, too much on his mind, worried about work, about the children, about the economy. I wish I had a nickel for every time I heard "It will be fine"; I could fly to Rio, well, OK, maybe Iowa. There are actually more available remedies for men than women. Shame to the man (or woman) who discourages his partner! Shame, shame! No one should be celibate unless they are monks, and hey, I don't think monks, priests and nuns should be celibate, either. They are human with the same human needs as the rest of us.

A woman may need to literally pick up the phone and make a doctor's appointment for her man. He may be paralyzed with fear himself and unable to acknowledge the issue. I let this go for far too long with one lover I had several years ago. It was always something: inability to get an erection, increased time to get an erection, inability to maintain an erection, premature ejaculation. Dear Lord, I have paid my penance on earth for my sins. *Enough suffering.* Stop the denial and get on the bandwagon to help yourself and him and save the intimacy of your relationship. That doesn't mean you should tactlessly hit him over the head with an exclamation: "Damn, baby, not again!" or even worse "It doesn't matter. Really." It *does* matter. He knows that and he knows you know it, too. Do something!

With or without the ability to have an orgasm, however, comes the need to be close to another human being in some special way.

If you want to spice up your sex life, you need to spice yourself up first. So here is my advice for perimenopausal through postmenopausal women:

Exercise is the great libido booster, don't kid yourself. Get off your duff and force yourself to go for daily long walks. Walking is easy, just one foot in front of the other, fun and free. Add on time each month and accelerate your speed. Get a buddy to do it with you. Measure and weigh yourself before you begin (*In other words, humiliate yourself in front of a friend who is humiliating herself in front of you.*).

Add other forms of exercise as you progress: biking, swimming, kayaking, dancing, hiking. Do what you enjoy but *do it more frequently.*

Attitude: *Improve your attitude.* You are not your mama. You have all the advantages of living in the 21st century, for Pete's sake. *You may age but you don't have to be old.*

Get a new haircut and color. Have a make up lesson (Update, update, update! This is not 1965: no bubble heads!).

Really critique your wardrobe (*Define yourself with fashion from the second decade of the new millennium*). When I got to Paris I realized I needed boots to fashion-survive. Then I realized all my pants were way too baggy, adding years to my age. Yikes! *Update the wardrobe!*

Nutrition. Pay attention to what you eat! (*Seriously, put down the Milky Way bars and have a kiwi!*) No, I am not a communist. Try to cut down on goodies and add lots of fresh vegetables to your plate.

Drink less booze, wine, beer. (*You may remember what happened the night before!*). It will help your focus, clarity, calorie count and you will feel better overall. Chug-a-lug more water.

Don't be afraid to *be sexy*. Maybe your grandmother wasn't; but it is not against the law. Now, in this time frame, attractive, well put-together, "hot" women are admired by both men and women. Even if you aren't Sofia Loren, you can be the best you can be, just like the Army. Are you really being that now? In Europe older women are considered sexy, *thank God.* Younger men go out of their way to meet them as I recently was witnessing, experiencing and enjoying but not if they are overweight and living in the past.

Start a new hobby that isn't illegal. Attend a lecture. Read a good book. Go bungee jumping. Join a new group (not an "all women's only" group) and cultivate yourself like the rose in full bloom that you are. You will become a more interesting person. You don't want a dull man, do you? Well, no man wants a dull woman, either.

Get sexual with yourself. Solo flying is better than being grounded. You have heard the phrase "Use it or loose it", haven't you? Well, that is a medically proven fact. The longer you have been in denial of your sexuality the more difficult it will be to recapture it. Try a vibrator, introduce yourself to new sex toys (it is *not* illegal or immoral). Taoists call it "self cultivation". Do you believe that? I love it! *Self-cultivation.* Go farm yourself!

Be a better communicator. Yeah, we women like to blame poor communications on men but honestly we are accountable, as well. I admit that I would break up with a decent guy who was a bad kisser rather than say anything. Hands raised: I am guilty. But no more. I haven't a clue about how many more years are left but I am not going to waste them by not communicating clearly with a man.

Do something you have always longed to do. Skydive, plan a biking adventure, hike in Tibet, learn a new language, take art lessons, join a Meet Up group, or volunteer to teach children in Africa. Consider the infinite number of possibilities! Grow! Then, if you so desire, reclaim your sexuality.

So, that brings us back to the first page of my story. I ran away from home, from men, depression, boredom, my crazy adult children and the economy. I made a conscience choice to awaken myself in a different culture, different country. All the ducks were waiting in a row: attention, affection, kissing, touching, communication, lovemaking and a renewed zest for life. They all still draw you nearer someone and that is a fact of life.

Nurturing may come in many forms. If sexual intercourse is not an answer for you, then there are other answers.

I remember one of my previously described lovers and I taking a long hot, steamy shower together. I washed and scrubbed him and as I was finishing soaping up his thighs I looked up and asked him "When was the last time you had this done for you?" "Never!" he grinned, enjoying every stroke. *And returning the favor is the law of successful relationships.*

Another lover long ago, Mel, who was clearly verging on impotency, knew how tired I was and offered to give me a massage. Now, lots of guys offer that and after five minutes want to forge on to new pursuits. But he did not. He spent a whole hour massaging me and the winning point here was that *he continued massaging me even after I fell asleep*. It was divine! It nourished more than my body and it made up for a whole lot of other things.

Nurturing a sense of closeness with one other person is one of the components for living a quality life. Do you really want to give up on that experience *for half a lifetime?!*

Seven

I loved seeing Paris through the eyes of the French. I loved hearing their voices. They could be nibbling on your neck and telling you, in French, they had to go home to their wife and three kids and yet it sounded fantastic. Ouh la la! But, I did see English-speaking men, as well.

Before I left the U.S., I had been contacted by an attorney from the East Coast, Wade, who was going to be there with his teenager attending school in Paris for a semester at the same time I was. Would I want to hang out occasionally? Sure! It is much more fun doing Paris with a friend. But, clearly, after meeting him in person this man was looking for a Friend With Benefits. Now, this guy not only had a wife but he also had a mistress back in the good, old US of A. Still, with his expectations high, he was looking for a leisurely diversion. Idiot. Maybe he was French in another life. Hell, he thought he was French in this life!

I wasn't interested but I wanted an American friend who I could bounce things off. Wade was that. It was interesting to compare notes with him. He wasn't exactly good looking but he had nice eyes, facial hair (I loathe facial hair) and a talent for knowing more about Paris than I. That wasn't so hard since we both knew he had lived there for a year. He spoke French and took the liberty of correcting mine constantly.

Wade was also a bit of a cheapskate to put it mildly. He never offered to pay so much as a drink for me. When I asked him about his girlfriends and mistresses, he said he rarely paid a tab for them either. Yuck! That sure would have turned me off *if I had been interested.* Here is a guy with a family income of more than $300K a year and he can't even treat his bed partners to dinner and wine? Would never work for me. But then, on all levels, Wade was not the one for me, anyway. Thank the Good Lord.

Once we went biking around the city and I swear, he wasn't really considering the fragility of my life. Up hills, down tiny, cobbled streets we pushed, irritating all the cars we blocked with our bicycles. Why he didn't stick to the main bike paths throughout Paris was beyond me. There were many miles of bike paths. I found Wade to be a narcissistic, egomaniac scrooge masquerading as a Frenchman.

I had never heard of the term "Hammam" before Wade. He wanted to go to one. Basically, they are Turkish baths but there are Hammams and there are Hammams. In some, there are ladies' days, men's days, couples days, and co-ed days. In others, they are naturists who parade around naked but allegedly don't indulge in any sexual conduct. That, of course, is where he wanted to go.

Nudity is not something that I am particularly interested in but I would find it easier to participate if everyone is a stranger. I have been to naturist habitats in Germany and Spain where their many spas offered legitimate co-ed, *non-sexual* saunas and steam rooms. I also had lived in Hawaii where there was a Nudist

Camp outside Honolulu on the North Shore. Thirty-five years ago, while living as a newlywed in Honolulu, I sold Tupperware. Mostly, it was a chance to socialize with other women. My husband was then an officer in the Navy and was not always around as much as I would have then preferred so I took up a part-time profession of Tupperware sales. When I got wind of this "nature camp" I thought they would be excellent targets for the Tupperware product line. They were living in tents on the beach, after all.

As a testament to my sales ability, I talked my virginal, Chinese Baptist girlfriend, Nancy, into going with me. We had been warned that we, too, would have to go nude. I thought I should get an award from Tupperware for this, like a Girl Scout Badge of Courage. Forward we went. We were sure we wouldn't know anyone or ever see these people again.

Poor, Nancy. I can still see her struggling with her modesty as both men and women gathered for the presentation. We actually ended up being allowed to wear small t-shirts, which we tried hard to pull down to cover the sacred places that so few (at least at that time) had ever seen. We got razed about that from a couple of the men.

Onward I progressed with my presentation, trying to be professional and avoiding looking below anyone's neck. But, Virginal Nancy could not. She had never seen a naked man in her life. Later, she said to me in wonder: "Did you see that guy in the front row? Did you see the size of his… of his…? OhmyGod, I had no idea!" Dear Nancy remained in the shock of the experience for some time.

I might be able to go to a co-ed Hammam with a lover but definitely not with the voyeur, Wade! I will be damned if he was going to have the distinct privilege of viewing my flat tushie, and saggy, little tummy. No thanks. A man needs to be fortified with either true love or undeniable lust to survive that erotic experience.

But I did want to go to a Hammam.

That would happen with another man: Jules. But, let's not get sidetracked...

I didn't see Wade too much after that.

I hardly ever saw Jules at night. He was a slave to the hotel industry or so he acted. He seemed so simply honest that I trust he was not involved with anyone else, although officially, within the context of our open relationship, he could do so.

Not all French are participants in the 35-hour workweek, six to eight week vacations with loads of holidays off in between. Jules, because he was so young to be managing a mid-size hotel, felt he had no right to complain, ask for days off or have any relief step in and help out. The keynote word here is "young". The job he worked normally was for someone with ten years of hotel experience. An older manager would not have put up for long with those endless hours and no chance for a private life. It is no wonder Jules had to find someone who was there to have fun, who didn't want any commitment, and to whom he was attracted.

Enter me.

One of the best things about Jules was he came prepared to take me someplace he thought I would like. This goes a long way for any of us who could not rely on a man to actually put time, thought and effort into taking us out. Often, we would go outside the city to visit a cathedral like St Gervais-St Portios in St Denis, where royalty are buried or Vaux-le-Vicomte, the Grand Chateau outside Paris, both of which I would never have visited if it weren't for him. He was thoughtful. He drove me here, there and all over the place to work out my needs in Paris. He really was essential to my early survival. My own Eagle Scout with Benefits. The worst thing about him was that he rarely arranged anything more than a day in advance. He was not a good communicator about his free time. Both drove me nuts as we fumbled along, trying to define our "relationship".

Being reserved, Jules didn't believe in PDA, public displays of affection. Yet, get me on that closet elevator up to my apartment and he was all over me. At first, I thought maybe it was because I was so much older and he didn't want to draw attention to us. But, as I got to know him it probably had nothing to do with age. In the car, he would reach out and touch my hand, or kiss me at a stoplight, and sometimes he would sneak a kiss on the back of my neck in a Cathedral but I learned not to expect more.

Interestingly, I was willing to accept him as he was, at least in the beginning. He would find out that I was imperfect, as well, and hopefully, be graceful about it, not run like the turkeys I have known in my life. It has always been annoying that men, when they have their first disagreement with a woman or when a new woman says something that reminds them of their ex-wife or ex-girlfriend, run. Run, run, run. See Dick run. Out the door, in the car. See Dick screech down the street. Never see Dick again. The End. I have met very few who see an argument through, forgive me my imperfections and love me all the same. Gads, I could be loyal to a guy who did that!

I never expected that a younger man could fill that role. It takes so much living, so many life experiences, so many mistakes and insight to be able to get over the bumps in a newly-forming relationship. The chances of that happening with a younger man were infinitesimal. Still, I was going with the flow and the river was running along at a good pace, thank you.

But there was more to life than this...

Eight

What makes for a good lover, anyway? Forgetting age factors, if each woman in the world could choose her ideal lover, what would she want? It's simple. Everything! We want them to romance us, to shake us so much to our core that we forget all common sense and moral code and throw open our bodies (literally and figuratively), tall and short, fat and thin, blemished and imperfect as we are and surrender to our knight. What a crock we buy into! Forget about Cinderella. Forget about being a Princess. Besides, we are not talking about a good husband here. We are talking about a good lover. The requirements are different.

I didn't have a sexually active marriage. For twenty-three years I waited for my husband to wake up to the joys of sex. But you can't transform a frog into a prince if he truly is a frog. A needlepoint pillow sits in the bedroom of my home, a gift from one of my sisters after my divorce. There is a frog on it that is wearing a crown. Stitched around the frog it begs the question: "Just how many frogs do I have to kiss before I meet my handsome Prince?" Good God, a lot, apparently! Over and over again I have met men who are open to discussing their former sexless marriages. *I have drawn the conclusion that love does not conquer all.* If a sexual person marries an asexual person there may well be mountains to climb in that marriage. Of course, when it's new and exciting almost everyone is interested –

or pretending to be interested in it – to attract a partner. We strut like peacocks luring in our mate. But similar, compatible sexual natures are an essential ingredient to a strong, lasting intimate relationship; eventually, any sexual incompatibility will rear its ugly head and guarantee the end of the relationship, officially or unofficially.

How can we be in a strong, intimate long-term relationship if there is no sex? While living under the same roof, sharing baby diapers, bills, farts, and dirty dishes but not fulfillment, the relationship dissolves. The loss is a loss of the quality of life. It is my belief that there are many, very many sexless or unfilled intimate relationships both in and outside marriage. The challenge is when one is sexual and the partner is not. Is that resentment I see heading over the hill in this direction? While there is a lot more to a successful relationship than sex it is still one of the most important parts of the equation. It is the binding agent in the recipe. It is the *balance* to the challenges life throws your way.

Beyond sexual compatibility, in marriage there needs to be life compatibility: similar value systems, life goals, personalities, style, hopes and commitments to keep the relationship alive till The Great Beyond. Otherwise, don't kid yourself. It won't work out in the long run (unless neither of you care about sex). A lover, outside of marriage, has different requirements. Having a lover doesn't necessarily mean a life commitment, does it? So let's go back to that all-important point: What makes for a great lover?

There was a man in my life, about a year after my divorce (when I was starving for physical affection after a long term hiatus of sex from my marriage) and I didn't care that he wasn't "Mr. Right". He was as sexual as I and there was a huge attraction between us. Nothing else. Just that. I admit I was aware of that so I can't say I expected more nor did I want more from him. There were just so many compromises I had to make because he wasn't my equal on any footing. But I also wasn't going to sell my soul to get laid. I wasn't pathetic, after all.

Men who think they are Great Lovers (and they usually brag openly about it) probably are not. It is all an exaggeration of promises usually unfulfilled leaving the recipient (women) disappointed. But, Mac and I were all over each other like bees on honey. Mainly I was relieved I still could respond like a woman, albeit a woman coming from a desert of celibacy. Mac had me up on my white grand piano once and he was all over me as I used my toes to create my own unique piano concerto. Mozart would be proud! God, it was sexy!

He was tall, lean, charming and a world-class athlete. He had more testosterone than anyone I have ever met. A very aggressive guy, he had the ability to attain, retain and regain an erection in two seconds flat (bless him for that, at least!). If there were a sexual Olympics he would have won the gold. That was what I needed at the time. He was also a creative lover. He tied me up once and then blindfolded me and took a carnation and caressed my body with it. Not many men think of doing those things. So, in creativity and energy, he got an A. If we could have lived our lives in bed we might have succeeded but nothing else held us together. He bordered the definition for "abusive". He took delight in embarrassing me in public and I cringed through it all because I was starved for sex.

I eventually grew not just tired of *but afraid of him*. It took me a long time to figure him out and when I did, a long time to get rid of him. After I did, he stalked me, broke into my home, took my boss out to lunch to gossip about me, called me constantly, sent mail endlessly and otherwise harassed me. I had been trusting, sincere, and forgiving even if I was needy, but still not desperate enough to stay with him. The truth shouted that we were not a match on any level.

Because of him I became a legal expert in several courts. I was introduced to family court and restraining orders, criminal court and civil court, all of which I won. Still, years later, I think about that freak who was convinced he was the Great White Lover and while the sex was sorely needed, it lacked in tenderness, equality, class and commitment. The man was a sociopath, I am positive. I still cringe at my bad judgment. It was all just a bombastic experience but perhaps, one I needed on my life resume. It helped me later appreciate the good guys. Even my ex was looking better.

There was another man, Tim, who I met on Easter morning on the steps of my church. I thought it was God-ordained. I was wrong. God had nothing to do with it; He was probably cringing Himself. Tim was a successful businessman, newly divorced (or so he said), wealthy and lived a mile away from me. He was attracted to the naiveté in me, I am sure. I told you that got me in trouble. But, he was a member of my congregation. How trustworthy could a person get? Still, there are men who prey on good women especially the naïve ones affiliated with churches.

Tim was about 6'5" tall, a big man, who as it turned out thought he was a gift to women by The Almighty. When we eventually landed in bed and became lovers, I was amazed and happy to see all things were, err...proportionate to his height. He knew it, too. He even alluded to it. Tim, even as well endowed as he was, actually avoided intercourse. *What the hell?* Here he was, fully capable but yet unwilling to satisfy his partner with intercourse. Fear of intimacy?

He is the only man I ever faked an orgasm with. What was I thinking?! He figured it out and called me on it. How friggin' embarrassing is that? Actually, it was funny, I laughed to myself later on. Guess I am not good at faking it. I had never faked it before and I would never do it again. It is such a colossal lie and counter-productive to anything a woman wants for herself. He thought he was a good lover by virtue of his size (as most large men believe). But he sorely lacked in most other areas and he preyed on good women who would be less suspicious of his erratic behaviors. The first time he kissed me he leaned back, opened his mouth like he was trying to catch flies and waited for me to lean over and kiss him. Hey, I am not a fly! I don't want to fall in to that deep cavern. I took my fingers and closed his mouth and gave him a gentle kiss. In hindsight, he was lucky I gave him that.

Turned out Tim was married although he protested that to the end. He was wealthy enough to have several homes. Jerk. *Who are these guys?* So much for "God-ordained"!

Neither Tim nor Mac was a good lover in the true sense of the term. They were emotionally unavailable and insincere and even though their stamina and size were of interest they lacked in all sorts of other things. Discouraging, isn't it?

A good lover treats a woman well before and after sex. No wham, bam, thank you mam's. Foreplay begins long before you hit the boudoir. There must be honesty and trust between lovers, understanding and agreement about the relationship. A good lover tries to fulfill your needs, whatever they may be. Unlike Adolph, a good lover gives and receives communication – *especially in bed* – like he/she thrives on it. Good lovers think equally of the partner and not just of themselves. Many of the same attributes of a long-term companion/spouse apply, just on a shorter basis of time. And whatever your agreement, be it exclusivity or not, a good lover faithfully abides by that *without judgment.*

Equality in bed is another important thing. Mac expected and loved oral sex but was hesitant to reciprocate the favor. *I beg your pardon?* After I explained that was fine but I wouldn't be obliging him if he weren't obliging me, he quickly changed his mind. *But why should anyone have to threaten their lover to get what they want?* If it is too one-sided it is not equal. Each partner should be eager to please and spend time with the other.

A few other desirable elements: good hygiene, good breath, dental hygiene (who wants to kiss someone with yellow teeth?) no diseases, some experience, OK, a *lot of experience,* preferably no pacemakers, ambulatory, enough time, the use of condoms, a good sense of humor, communicative and creative.

I put the question out to some women , many of them, admittedly young, and this is how they responded:

"Take your time! I probably have other things on my mind, like kids, groceries, bills, obligations. I need to have you siooooow down and let me get in the swing of it." That sentiment was echoed by all.

"Manscaping is a must!!!! (What the hell was that, I wondered). Nothing ruins a mood more than pubic hair in my mouth…eeeeewwww." Everyone has dealt with that over the years, but what was this "manscaping" thing she referred to, exactly? I checked with this woman to find out that younger people all over are trimming their pubes these days for that very reason of access and comfort. In my age bracket, they are lucky to still have a few hairs…anywhere beyond the ears, nose and eyebrows (like Andy Rooney they refused to groom their hair…wherever it is).

On the list went:

"I like to be in charge more often …but if you relax and roll with it, I'll blow your mind." (Hmmm. I bet she taught him a thing or two.)

"I need some space to move around and it doesn't always feel good with your body weight bearing down on me."

"Be creative. I get bored easily."

"I like to tell you what I need. I know you are not a mind reader...so don't get all flustered and your "manhood" dented (no pun intended) if I need it somewhere or somehow differently."

"I vary by mood. Sometimes I don't like to talk. Sometimes I do. Sometimes I like to be demure. Sometimes not...it's in the spirit of fun." (*She wouldn't have been a match for Adolph.*)

"I love creative experimentation. Change the location, time of day, lighting, situations, positions."

"Cuddling is good, but don't hang all over me all night long. I need my space."

"Keep your tongue OUT of my throat. Porns are not real. They are shot for good camera angles." (*That reminds me of my "propeller kissing date. I'll tell you about him later.*)

 "Someone who takes out the garbage without being asked."

Like I said before: what do women want? Everything! So, what's the problem?

But, of course, you agree; there is more to life than this...

Nine

A few days after my date with Jules, after his breakthrough statement of intentions, his proposition, his declaration, his negotiations for a sex partner (gads, that *still* sounds awful, doesn't it?) we went out again. This time he took me up the hills of Montmartre. It is a lovely, hilly and eclectic area and it was another beautiful autumn day in Paris. All of a sudden, his face changed. He looked somber, almost sick. Of course, I bit at it. I accepted that he had worked well into the night at some function at his hotel and was up again early the next morning.

"What is it? What's the matter?" I asked him, concerned.

"Nothing. I am just very tired. I would like to take a short nap and rest for a little bit."

"Are you feeling alright?"

"Yes, I am just very tired."

"Well, do you want to take a nap in your car and I can walk around for a half hour and then come back?"

"No, no. Let's just go back to your place where I can lie down."

Hmmm. Frankly, I was a little suspicious and irked that he wanted to return home so quickly. Hey, I was taking a tour, for God's sake! Is nothing sacred?

But I wanted to give him the benefit of the doubt so back we drove to my place. I led him into the bedroom and returned to sit in the living room and read a book. Immediately, I heard him call my name.

"Tasha…"

I went to him.

"Come lay down here next to me," he said, already under the covers. Hmmm.

I declined. "You get some rest" I remarked, irritated that I now fully understood the premise of getting me back here in this not very veiled attempt.

Well, one thing, of course, led to another. What was I holding out for, anyway: hell to freeze over? Hadn't I already grown my virginity back with a celibate life? I wasn't getting any younger. Didn't I always fantasize about a lover in Paris? Yada, yada. So I acquiesced to the moment. I surrendered. I let him have his way with me. I handed over, if not my soul, my bod and gave him all I had. After all, the idea of dying with Adolph as my last lover was still appalling!

I don't know how many times I have actually had a *young* lover. Of course, Brett had only been twenty-two and my husband was only twenty-three when we married, but Brett and I were cautiously gentle because it was my first time. My husband was living in an old body as well as an old soul so that was not always thrilling. Really I was a little flattered and thrilled to see the enthusiasm Jules displayed. What a difference, praise the Lord, between Jules and the older men I had experienced. What a joyful, lovely, wonderful difference! I forgave him his little lie, I can tell you that much. He was hardly "tired".

But here is what I had to come to terms with: taking on a new lover and still having the freedom to go out and date others. I didn't really know how well that would work for me. Could I take on two lovers, for instance? I mean, would he get territorial? Would I get guilty? We Christians carry guilt around everywhere. So how I would react to dating beyond Jules, *while we were lovers,* was yet to be determined. I had never been involved in a relationship that had not been monogamous. This would be a first. I wondered if I could pull it off. Jules was correct. I needed to go out and have fun while I was in Paris and he would be too busy to enter into an exclusive relationship. I *never* want to sit at home waiting, like I did throughout my marriage, for my man to come home. Never again!

So, I continued to go out and meet men. It was rather cool, this freedom to do what I wanted. That I admit. But it bothered me when Jules wanted to hear everything about my dates. It is hard to discuss a date you had the night before as you relax in post coital bliss. It was not my intention, either, to make him jealous.

Once I had a date I was meeting at Les Halles cinema and Jules and I went out beforehand. We had such a great time and I didn't want to part although I knew he had to go to work. But he was very concerned and unhappy with where this man wanted to meet. Les Halles has a rough, young crowd especially in the evening and there are swarms of police monitoring but he didn't like it. He insisted on actually walking over to the place I was to meet this man! How awkward is that? Later, he realized, I was not going out with my American acquaintance, Wade, but had a date and apologized. But clearly he was concerned about my safety. I don't remember anyone ever being concerned about my safety. It was rather dear.

I didn't want to introduce him to this new man. After I urged him to leave, he hugged and kissed me and warned me to be careful. I looked back at him as he left and he was watching me. I didn't even want to go out with this new man; I wanted to be with Jules. Yet, here I was leaving my lover for another man with his blessing. Who'd a thunk?

It was September 16 and I was about to endure my most boring date- thus far - in Paris. I turned around to look for him. I had been sent his photo through Craig's List. Yeah, I was becoming Queen of Craig's List. But let me mention something here. I was very cautious, screened everyone I communicated with, exchanged photos and always met in a public place, usually under the Eiffel Tower (This meeting was the exception.). There are weirdoes on Craig's List but there are also decent people. I am one of them (the latter). I never gave out my home address either before meeting someone. I normally went out with someone a couple of times before I decided if I wanted them to know where I live (with the one exception of Pierre). I always talked to them on the phone prior to meeting them and eliminated some that way, as well. No one should take risks. And from what I heard from men, there were some creepy women, as well as prostitutes on Craig's List. So I went about it cautiously.

I walked ten feet and there was my date, Jacques. Honestly, that was his name. How French can it get? Jacques was about thirty-five years old, not particularly good looking but very stylishly dressed. His one prominent feature was his lips. They were huge, the size of The Holy Roman Empire. They sort of jutted out so you could see part of the inside lip moisture. I couldn't get my eyes off them. If you lined up a hundred men the only way I could identify Jacques was by his mouth. The rest of his face was non-descript. I couldn't imagine being kissed by those lips. A girl could get swallowed by that mouth. It was dangerous, the entrance into an abyss. I wondered to myself if there was such a thing as lip reduction surgery. If there were, he clearly would be a good candidate for it. Obviously, I would never go out with Mick Jagger, even if he, kneeling before me, arms outstretched, begged me. *Desole,* Mick.

Basically, Jacques was a computer geek. That had a certain allure for me, however, because I endlessly need help with my computer issues. Where women once strived to meet doctors and lawyers, they now jumped at the opportunity to meet a man who could fix their computer. I was no exception. But Jacques, well *Jacques was really a full-fledged geek.* He had *no* people skills. He had *no* idea of how to behave on a date with a woman. And he was a cheapskate. Never, ever in my life have I gone to any fast-food chain for a dinner date. I hate fast food. I am a proud card-carrying foodie. I live and breathe good cuisine. I am a culinary adventurer, who has tried everything from stuffed cow intestines to rattlesnake. I trained in France and Italy in professional culinary schools. I was a food editor, a cooking teacher. I despise crappy food. OK, message received.

I am surprised I didn't say "No" to the food. I was trying to be kind. *Mistake.* I knew immediately there would be no second date; I should have suggested a normal restaurant. Yuck, what an awful, dirty, horrible place it was there in the Les Halles mall. I drank my orange juice (they had no liquor license) and barely touched my food, which is probably why I survived. He didn't seem to notice. He didn't have much of a personality. I took the initiative with the conversation. Being an Irish American I have the gift of the gab; I could talk to an elephant easily so taking on this young man in conversation was no big deal. Except: boring! Boring the kiss of death for me.

We went to a "special showing" with a cinema group. The cinema was a surprise and unnamed until everyone was seated. He didn't tell me there would be a long lecture in French beforehand. I understood one word and for forty-five minutes listened to three pretentious French "producers" talking gibberish. It was all I could do not to take flight and run out the door. I felt sorry for the kid. He clearly had no appreciation that he was out with the Queen of Craig's List!

Finally, mercifully, the movie began. It was an old Jimmy Stewart movie "Mr. Smith Goes to

Washington", which I have seen several times. It was in English, at least, but not exactly what I wanted to see. Still, I practiced being classy. I do practice that every now and then just to throw people off. I stayed, bored to death as I was, and couldn't wait to get out of the theatre. Afterwards, he wanted to go to a reception.

"They are giving a free glass of wine and appetizers" he implored me, as if a cheap glass of wine and a mile-long queue of people pushing for a free bite at something would surely convince me to stay. It didn't. I had better wine at home but he was intent on staying whether I liked it or not. He made that clear.

I turned and started to walk away but thought better of it. I went back to him and told him quietly, politely "Please do not call me again. You are not a gentleman" and I huffed off, relieved at getting away from him at last. He might have offered to walk me downstairs and see that I get on the metro safely. Instead, he was trying to get his freebies. Get me out of here! I can't breathe! Where is my dear, sweet Jules when I want him?

Home I went. But, that was the worst of it. The most boring date in Paris on this trip (at least for the ones who showed up at all) so I can't really complain. Boredom is just a misdemeanor, not a felony. But, as I stated earlier, it is, for me, the kiss of death to a relationship.

My Jules was horrified when I told him. "He took you *where*?!" he retorted indignantly, more upset than I was (bless him). There are other restaurants that are not expensive in the mall but clearly this Jacques guy was unwilling to fork over any euros. He really knew how to impress a girl! Jules told me I should have left and couldn't understand why I stayed. I didn't want to hurt the kid's feelings, basically. He was in way above his head with me that was for sure. Jules marveled at my kindness even if the geek didn't. So I guess it served a purpose.

Ten

Almost from the beginning with Jules it was a constant adjustment. I had to call upon my maturity, my life experiences and my knowledge of men to adjust to how he wanted to act out our parts on the stage we call life. "All of life is a stage" wrote Shakespeare, "and each must play his part." I wonder if Shakespeare knew any Frenchmen. Because Jules insisted we have an open relationship, the day after our first romp in bed I went back to Craig's List and put an ad up. Guess who answered it? Yep, Jules! He didn't know it was I from his remarks. I just sat there stunned, shocked, disappointed, hurt and angry all in one fell swoop and not just at him but at me. Well, that put everything in its place, didn't it? I knew, of course, right from the start that I was never going to have a long term relationship with him but good Lord Almighty, I had just handed over my sacred body to his pleasure (OK, mine, too) to find out he was still shopping! My, my, my. How humbling dating can be.

I didn't answer that email. I didn't respond to his next email sent directly to me. I had to think about it. Look, I say the guy was honest right from the start. I was almost glad to find this out….almost, but I was going to talk to him about it. And I did.

He sat across the table from me and he sensed something was wrong. I asked him just to let me "get it all out" before he commented. On I babbled for some ten minutes straight. He seemed to get it, although in hindsight I may have sounded like the grandmother I am. I had said no to everyone for years until I met Jules. I was a privilege he ought to appreciate. Why would he jump back on the investigative trail so quickly after such a new encounter? When a women opens her body to a man it is sacred....yada, yada, yada. I will say this for him. He didn't laugh. He had the good sense to let me talk and to acknowledge my feelings. He had the intelligence to show contrition and apologize and promise to do better. Gads, if more men knew how to have such a disagreement there would be fewer disagreements. I forgave him but it forever reminded me (in case I drifted into illusions) that this was, indeed, a very *temporary* alliance, nothing more.

The trouble with sex, or the privilege of it, is that it is a way for two people to bond that they don't do with other people. It tends, and it should, to bring two people together in a unique way. It is difficult to have other relationships when one is evolving in an intimate way. But this was Paris. This was the *reality* of Paris. It would not be my life forever. I was just learning to play the game at a late stage of life. Some of it was still very exciting.

Continually, young men were approaching me on the internet. It was amazing to me that so many young men want older women. Older men didn't seem to want us. So, as I have said before, I was learning to go with the flow. Not everyone I met wanted me in any way, I humbly inject. But, thank God, there weren't too many of those.

I met Jean Louis under the Eiffel Tower as we had planned through our Craig's Listing communiqué. He was suave, sophisticated, a part time actor. We went for a glass of wine nearby and he was charming. But it became apparent that Jean Louis was intent on meeting someone who could build a family life. Why he answered an ad that declared I was in my fifties (just a fib, not a lie. Women are expected to fib about their age, aren't they? It is not a sin.), who knows. We parted on good terms and I didn't hear from him again. *Nes pas problem.*

There were other young men applying for the job. But one can sense their maturity level by the way they correspond. I found myself telling them the truth: "I am too old for you. Look for a younger woman. We don't have enough in common." "Finish Kindergarten first." Anyone, any age who referred to himself as "Dude" is a pass for me. Another lad kept emailing me, calling me a "hot babe". I signed my response, "Hot Babe Grandma"). I was being a protective grandma to all the young birds who wanted to jump out of the nest and try their wings or jump *into* my nest. And I was having fun in the process.

But there was more to my life than this…

Eleven

In late September I found out there would be a half marathon race from the Eiffel Tower to Versailles. I decided to seize the moment and hurried to a local doctor to receive the required medical authorization. I promptly registered for the race, having no idea what to expect. Jules, as always the thoughtful chauffeur, whisked me over to headquarters to pick up my runners' packet a few days beforehand. He was always finding the time to do those types of things. I loved that about him.

I decided to spend the next two weeks before the race in early morning training. On that first training session I stepped from my apartment door at five in the morning to be greeted by a cold, dark, foggy Paris morning. I rather liked the fog; it gave a new mystique to my beautiful Paris. I circled my arrondissement dressed in runner's leggings and a tank top. I planned for my first training to be two hours long. That seemed do-able.

I actually enjoyed the darkness that blanketed early morning Paris. It wasn't something I often experienced. In the fifteenth arrondissement there is a mix of old and new architecture. While I adore the old buildings I must admit that I found the odd-shaped new buildings along the Seine quite intriguing. On I hurried. Savory aromas whiffed by me from the opening boulangeries, piping with their hot croissants and breads.

By the time I reached the Tower, silhouettes, like morning ghosts, of other athletes started to appear.

On I hastened in the early morning sun, fog rising above a now sunny Eiffel Tower, quite an extraordinary sight to see. Warmly dressed passersby stared at me incredulous at the minimal amount of clothing I had on. I could almost hear them say to each other of my attire, "But that is absurd; it is freezing out here!" But with my exercising I was toasty warm.

I was eager enough to think I could have done another two hours. Good thing I didn't. My first training session turned out to be my last training session. Almost immediately I felt blisters all over my toes. I am not a runner. I am a fast walker. It is a better sport, healthier with less trauma to the joints. But I hadn't enough time to train if I let my blisters heal. Then I SKYPEed my sister about my poor, aching feet. She warned me: "Stay off your feet and get rid of the blisters. You have strong legs. You don't need to train." It was good advice. So, good little former Catholic that I am, I did as I was told.

The day of the race arrived. Sunday morning I hurried out of my apartment, stretched, and then walked the few blocks to the Eiffel Tower, where twenty thousand athletes from around the world were warming up. It is about eighteen kilometers from the Eiffel Tower to Versailles. I viewed the video of the run on the website before I registered and wished I hadn't. It appeared as long as a marathon, and for that, one *really* needs a good amount of appropriate training. I had no training other than my daily walks around Paris although I had completed, in good time, a marathon a decade earlier for Leukemia's Team in Training in Alaska.

So there I was, an American in Paris, roaring to go, and off I jolted when the gun was shot. Honestly, I was the only speed walker in the masses of thousands of runners. I felt no matter how fast I hurried that I was standing still. They poured passed me. Still, their speed actually motivated me to go faster. Down streets, up, up endless hills, through towns, forests and tunnels my two chubby, little thighs hurried. It was a glorious day. The sun was brilliant. There was only one thing missing: port-a-potties. In the whole competition, I saw only *two* of them. Men just stepped four feet from the runners and splurted out across the bushes. Do they have no modesty? Apparently, not. I think the women had amazing control. I never once saw a woman stop to urinate anywhere. It amazed me because, of course, you drink water all along the course.

Onward, upward over them thar hills we all hurried. A few more hills than I expected, but damn, I told everyone I was doing this; I couldn't stop now. I have some pride! Especially gratifying was the fact that as runners began to slow down, I, the solo walker, hustled passed them. My "pleasure sensors" as my shrink called them, were alive and zinging all around me. My Nitric Oxide level was soaring!

Jules thought it would take me at least five or more hours. "I've tried it with my father once" he said. "It was a lot of work!" He was flabbergasted when I told him I did it in less than two and half hours. I was mighty pleased with myself. I love showing off (I can't help it, as I said before, I am an Aries.). My dear Jules, remember, was an old soul in a young body.

I was sixty-three, had a young Parisian lover and I was doing a half marathon - without training – and finishing in half the time it took him to finish! That, folks, is as good as it gets. I never stopped smiling. It was a captivating moment in my life to realize that so many goals and dreams were coming true.

At the end of the race I received a medal placed around my neck. I love that medal. It symbolizes to me that we should never discount ourselves just because we are older. There are still so many things to realize and the fun of that is in the planning. *Anticipation is everything.* Most of us are going to end up in the same place at the end; the journey is what is important.

But there was more to my life than exercise…much more…

Twelve

When I was a preteen I never could imagine how *anyone* could ever tell their boyfriend when they had their menstrual period. How horrifying to share such personal information with a boy! In my teens when I heard that my girlfriends told their boyfriends, again I was aghast. *So personal*. But, then I was a virgin till I was twenty-one. I had no experience with that type of relationship or intimacy with a boy. So, at my ripe old age, with experience galore behind me, I found I had no secrets. Don't hold back telling a man what you like. Relax. He probably will like it, too. My relaxed, uninhibited spirit certainly helped to relax my partners. I am proud of that, if truth be known.

So, it was during our second sexual encounter that I whipped out my favorite, (ah, what shall I call it?)...my little *gadget* that so many women knew about decades before me and showed it to Jules. He wasn't surprised; clearly, he had seen them before. "I want to show you exactly where it is happening for me." At which time, I showed him where I was the most sensitive (I called it "My Secret Garden"). I didn't want him to waste his time elsewhere if he were trying to induce an organism for moi. Hey, I ain't getting any younger! I don't want to waste my time, either. The Grim Reaper might be headed in my direction for all I know!

I didn't get my first little gadget till I was fifty. OK, so I am a late bloomer (but I sure am blooming now!) Gadgets can enhance sex. I used it on him and introduced positions that we could both feel it at the same time. You see, I amused him, as well.

He was amazed that something so small could be so powerful.

"Size is not everything" I pointed out to him *(it all about number of batteries!)*.

But how important is size? Men take a lot of crap about this. I declared, stupidly, to my sisters once many years ago that size didn't matter. What matters is how a man moves. Hmmm. Well, my sisters burst out laughing and simultaneously looked at each other and said: "Then you never had a small one!" What did I know? I guess at the time, I didn't. But be patient. Wait. A small one is coming your way and it ain't fun.

I met a decent guy on a cruise once. When we returned home we started to date. He admitted to me he had never had another woman other than his ex-wife. Hmmm. My girlfriends urged me to go to bed with him (I was still conservative about these things in those days, not so long ago.) "Well", I responded "either one of two things is going to happen here: either he will be an eager beaver student of mine or he will be a dud, too petrified to get with the agenda."

In a way, I was a little more turned on because at this point of my life I was confident and willing to teach him. But, and that is a big BUT, where the hell was it? I got no reaction from him when I was touching him.

There was barely a lump in his pants. Uh oh. Finally, we got to bed and he was on top (of course) and I still didn't know if he was in me, for heaven's sake! Only by looking up at him and the expression on his face did I realize he was, in fact, inside. He was just too small to feel. Discouraging. He had Teacher of the Year, a future Queen of Craig's List and he was the size of a lipstick. Lipstick would have been better; it is harder.

So, on this God-awful lesson went. Oral sex: He was willing to do it but didn't want me to do it. I immediately figured out he just didn't want me to see the size of his jewels. *OK, I thought, then you can just give me pleasure. No problemo!* In all fairness to the men in the world with ah, ah…how shall I put this….*small endowments*, it takes an act of courage for them to reveal their little (no pun intended) secret. It would be very difficult for them to take on a lover, fearing the worse: recognition of their pint-size package. And if I say nothing else here, as we stumble our way through these experiences, women everywhere need to be sensitive and considerate when they meet a man like this. In other words, don't yell out "Oh, Christ, is that all you have?" and jump up out of bed. It might be cause for a justifiable homicide. Yours.

Jules had no such problems. We were fairly well matched in bed as far as sexual interests go. We were both always interested in screwing. What do we call this, BTW? Love-making sounded a whole lot better to me but, as he pointed out, it was inaccurate (couldn't he have just been more politically correct? Nope, my independent youngster called it like he saw it.) So screwing, fucking, sucking were the general vernacular spoken in bed. For me, it would have been much more preferable to have him just start seducing me rather than breezily saying: "I want to fuck you". Now, occasionally, an "I want to fuck you" can be a turn on but not when it is said in the same tone as "I have to go to the bathroom" or "Get me a drink of water, would you?" It is the tone in the voice whispered in the dark that is a turn on. But honestly, I, with my years of experience, was a more evolved sexual person. I understood and embraced the subtleties of sex, the sensuality that should be there, even the erotic pleasures. He brought forth the energy, abilities and enthusiasm I so craved so I was not about to start complaining about vocabulary. Can you blame me?

I was always relieved that he insisted on safe sex and that he could go to it for a long time without any problems. No E.D. No pre-mature ejaculation. And then he would stop for a rest for both our sakes and get a new condom and start in again. Holy Schmoly that was fun.

I can remember once discussing the age difference (he never really knew my age) and he told me I was making an issue where no issue existed, smiled sweetly and squeezed my hand (it killed my arthritis but was sweet, nonetheless). Then, we were in the dining room at the time, he stated: "You look forty. Except when you disagree with me; then you look forty-five." I would have happily accepted forty-five. Then he added: "When we are screwing, you look thirty and when you are sucking me, you look twenty." Oh, yes, we may not have used the same terms, but, damn it, he made me laugh.

He did try to guess my age, though, another time. I had listed my age on Craig's List as "50s"). "Tell me", he asked "Fifty?... Fifty-One?... Fifty Two?" After going up the ladder and my repeated denials that he would ever know, he gave up. Wonder what he would have said if I responded "Sixty Three"? Older than his mum.

I had to go to the pharmacy and buy some lubrication. He provided the condoms, he declared. I had to go get whatever it was I needed beyond that. I asked to speak with the female pharmacist, who had served me before when I first arrived and she handed over the goods with a funny look on her face. I knew she wanted to say something, so I said it for her (beaming, of course). Yep, I had need of this. I had a new, young lover, I whispered to her, obviously delighted. She lit up.

"How young?" she whispered back, curious. "Forty," I responded, because that was before I knew Jules was thirty. I thought the woman was going to split her gut open trying not to laugh. She was delighted for me. "And I can give you a senior discount!" she laughed, knowing my age. "Enjoy!" she waved to me as I left the store. Both of our eyes were sparkling. I wish Jules had a brother; I would have shared him with her.

Enthusiasm: nothing like it. One night, Jules in his more passionate state, actually broke the bed beneath us as we did our thing. We started to laugh and completed our endeavors on a crooked bed, which brought blood flow to the head and made me a little dizzy. It was my first sex "injury". The entire environment was perfect: rain pelted against the windows. The symbolism wasn't lost on me. It was all marvelous. Glorious, really.

Let's go to a Hammam together, he stated. OK. Let's go. I had no idea what type of Hammam he was referring to and that another unique, risqué experience was promising to unfold.

Thirteen

I ran around a lot in Paris. I submerged myself into art. I immersed myself into music. I attended lectures, the ballet, the museums and the opera. That is the reason I was in Paris, and I certainly needed a rest every now and then from my new er...er...er sex partner (see, I still don't want to call it that.) I went to every museum that had impressionist art. I attended tours of areas and museums I hadn't known existed. I discovered all those chocolatiers and indulged myself. My senses could not have been more alive. My Nitric Oxide kept elevating, elevating, elevating!

Even my visits to the open-air marketplace near my home were fun. The variety of people, of foods, of products offered a spectacular people-watching opportunity. It was several visits before I realized that the farmer who sold the roosters and hens was the one who made the rooster noises. He was referred to as "The Rooster Man". I stood in front of him and laughed. He did, too. It was all so different from what I experienced daily at home in California.

My sister came for a visit. On her first full day, at Jules's expressed wishes, he, she and I all went on one of his walking tours. He wanted to meet her. "How will your family react to me?" he asked beforehand. "My sisters? Hell, they are probably jealous!" I laughed. In his modest little car, he took us all over, dressed in a business suit, to help my sister see part of his Paris. We stopped for crepes and ended up at my apartment where I had made coq au vin for us before we left.

"Clearly, Jules is in love with you" my sister remarked after he left.

"You think so?" I wondered back.

"Yeah. He just looks at you with that look. It is really very sweet." It was but I didn't want anyone getting hurt, either. What was my responsibility to him?

As I continued to go out with other men, Jules admitted across wine glasses one evening that he was just a "little bit" jealous. "But" he hastened to add "that is my problem, not yours." I told him we had to stop discussing other men. I was uncomfortable with it and it really was none of his business. He is the one who sent me out into the world to continue dating men. So I did, but from that moment forth I tried never to bring up a date again. I discouraged him from doing likewise, and all was well…. for a while.

Sex does bring you together, though. It is hard not to feel closer to someone you are in a sexual relationship. But we were friends. We truly enjoyed each other's company. I trusted no one in Paris more than I trusted Jules. He had an endearing, protective nature to him that I will never forget. But we were allegedly sex partners not lovers, remember. I threw that back at him every now and again because he never alluded to love in our relationship.

Once, however, we drove down to a popular and historic restaurant, Le Coupole and were talking as we walked towards the restaurant. "So you do have feelings for me?" I asked.

"Oui! Of course, I do. I have a great amount of feelings toward you." He wrestled with the thought and then blurted it out: "I would marry you if I could!" Shut my mouth.

Marry me? He didn't really think about that, did he? Still, it did show the depth of his feelings. He was just too reserved to say what he was feeling. Marriage would never be on the agenda. I had already been married and put one young man through medical school and a five-year residency, I was not about to build up Jules's career at a time I wanted someone to take care of me. That was never going to happen. Still, I was relieved to find that our relationship meant something to him and that he had strong feelings for me. I really didn't need more than that.

Flabbergasted at what he just told me, I sauntered into the restaurant with him feeling a little giddy. The feeling was as delicious as the oysters and foie gras.

Le Coupole, a cavernous, typical brasserie opened in 1927 and frequented by such luminaries as Dali and Picasso, was brimming with life and conversation. Deco murals adorned walls and the ceiling. We were squeezed into a table almost touching the adjacent tables to our left and right. It was hard not to hear everyone's conversation.

The couple to my left was clearly sexually involved. The man, a Frenchman, spoke openly to us about their relationship. She, a Canadian, was a married woman he was trying to woo away from her husband. Unembarrassed, she giggled and nodded in agreement. He spoke in French to Jules. Speaking in another language that precludes me always makes me uncomfortable. When I am being deliberately left out of the conversation, I find it rude. Eventually, this man offered to trade partners for a night! Holy Moly! I quickly discarded what he said, alluded to already being with a wonderful man, and tried not to talk to them after that. Later, Jules told me the man was talking in French about English women and how easy we were to figure out. Jules said he hated guys like this and was very uncomfortable in that moment. As always, he remained the perfect gentleman himself.

We returned home eventually, having fully recovered from the tacky couple and began to work out our fantasies. It was another wonderful, rainy night as we snuggled into bed.

But, as you know by now, there was more to my life that this...

Fourteen

So what happens when you meet another man? How confusing was my situation to get now? I don't remember who answered whose ad, but again, through Craig's List, Nick and I met. My guess is that he was in his mid 50's. He wore glasses, and looked like a cross between actors Robin Williams and Josh Lyman. He was a well-employed consultant, divorced with two kids who visited every other weekend. Our chemistry was fairly instantaneous. Nick had a wonderful sense of humor, sparkling eyes and an intelligence that I found charming. He was also more my equal than Jules, by virtue of his age and life experience. He appeared somewhat normal or normal as men get in Paris. I gravitated towards his sexual energy and he mine. Like a helpless insect that is compelled to the porch light bug zapper, I walked right into his life wholeheartedly – or should I say foolhardy? We all go blind when we have that type of connection.

After meeting for drinks we walked over to the Seine and watched the Eiffel Tower light show. I loved doing this and enjoyed it regularly. It was a beautiful autumn evening. Masses of people were out. We grabbed a chocolate crepe and sighed. Nick's hands were all over me. So I grabbed them playfully and held them in a safe position. I didn't want to rush into anything. I was fully in the moment. I could tell he wanted to kiss me but I told him not to. "Anticipation is everything" I reminded him, smiling and reluctantly he agreed.

But I couldn't wait to see him again.

Nick was a fairly good communicator...or so I thought at the time. When he got back to his home he sent me a lovely email thanking me for a great evening and telling me he wanted to see me again. It was signed "lots of kisses". The men in Paris are very expressive in that way. Loads of kisses, very flowery and romantic, praising and exalting your wonderful persona. I can't imagine an American men sending it to begin with... He had my attention. So, OK, I was listening!

Since he had his children that weekend, we planned on the following weekend. Something wonderful happens when your life is full. You don't depend on that call from a man to fill it. I had Jules. I had other dates. I had my tours, races, Meet Up groups, hiking groups, my music and the arts. I could wait. I wasn't biting my fingernails. Had I not been doing all those activities I would have watched the clock tick away eight days and nights till our date. I hate waiting to be asked out and while I am slowly, verrryyyyy sloooooowly, learning to take some initiative in the contacting of a man, I still tend to expect the man to take on that responsibility. Otherwise, I don't feel a guy is interested enough. After all, he should have more testosterone than I. I am the woman; at least, the last time I checked I was.

So we meet again first for drinks and then dinner. It was another magical night. Everything we did was connected. We each knew we were each interested. We relaxed at the café over a glass of wine and talked. Then we headed over to a landmark restaurant in Paris called Au Pied de Cochon. It so happens I had been to this restaurant seven years earlier with a boyfriend who took me to Paris for New Year's Eve week. We had stumbled upon it quite by accident. It was a miserably cold week in Paris with snow and ice abundant. Nobody was out on the streets. It was a great opportunity to take photos of some beautiful snow-laden buildings sans people and traffic. This restaurant is done in the Belle Epilogue style from the turn of the century-1893-1913. Stylish lamps and a bustling crowd might have been fodder for a postcard from Paris. Wonderful aromas from the kitchen assailed us as we took refuge on that snowy day.

All we ordered was a bottle of wine and two bowls of their "world-famous" French Onion Soup. It was all perfect: snow flakes danced against the windows, Jack Frost nipped at the door (I could write a song!), we at a leisurely place had nowhere to go and nothing to do. Regardless of the snow the restaurant overflowed with customers.

So, this, the second time I approached Au Pied de Cochon I was even more thrilled. Now, it looked like a Hollywood set, a sort of replica of itself. The windows were all gone and the restaurant opened out to a lovely terrace with tables, chairs, candlelight and green bushes to separate the customers from the pedestrians. Tradition continued: Same candelabras, same noisy restaurant, and same surly waiters.

Au Pied de Cochon, as the name implies, specializes in pig. Nick ordered a bottle of red wine and we talked. Frankly, when I am bursting with happiness I am my most charming self. My sense of humor is off the Richter scale. I am a magnate thanks to high Nitric Oxide levels. I couldn't believe I was back in this quaint restaurant with another man having another fabulous experience.

Somewhere during the early evening I put my lip balm on because I was prone to having dried lips.

"You don't need to do that" Nick smiled at me. "Your lips are perfect". (I love Paris. Have I said that before?)

"And I want to keep them that way or I won't get a kiss good-night". Sassy, little broad, aren't I?

"So " he now smiled fully, assured that at least this night he was going to get a kiss, "you are already thinking about it?"

"Oui! And you should be happy to know that!" I bantered back. Then, spontaneously, I continued "As a matter of fact I can't wait. Come over here" I leaned over the table "and kiss me right now!"

He happily obliged, relieved, perhaps, to see I was in fact, uninhibited. BTW, it was sort of fun, this being in charge of the kiss thing. It certainly added to the evening and relaxed me almost as much as the bottle of vin.

After we finished our dinner (he had pigs ears, snout and tail and I, wisely, had duck), we left, and walked around the neighborhood a bit. Nick (now encouraged, of course) would grab my arm and pull me off to a private alcove and start kissing me. Damn, he was a good kisser. (We will talk about kissing in another chapter. Stay tuned.) It was all so devil-may-care and such a perfect evening. Savor those moments because one never knows how long they will last.

We departed at the metro. I went in one direction, he in another. By the time I had gotten home, he had sent me another email, sweet and romantic.

Now, I thought, what was I going to do? "Torn Between Two Lovers", well, OK, he wasn't a lover yet, but gee I sure hoped he would be. Was I now being unfaithful to "my" Jules? Had Jules really expected me to date other men when he suggested it?

Back to emailing my sisters: "So can I have two lovers in the same time frame?" I questioned them. The answer came as it was up to me. No shit. That much I knew.

I promised myself to slow down with Nick until I got a better idea of where this could lead, hopefully in a magical place far away from heartache.

We next met at my apartment. He had invited me out for a cup of tea and I suggested it would be easier to just have tea at my place. He grabbed at the opportunity. It was a huge tactical error on my part. It was our third date, the one that many observe (but not me, usually) as the "Go" sign for bedding down with someone. Well, hell, I certainly didn't plan on doing that and I should not have invited him over knowing the heightened security alarms were there when it came to chemistry. Yet, I did.

I thought I was safe. I had another date that evening so I knew he would have to leave early. I think he had plans at the time, as well. Then, after tea, we both decided to cancel our respective plans. I whipped up some omelets and we opened a bottle of wine. It was an unpretentious, comfortable, candle-lit dinner in my dinning room. It is what we might have done had we been mar......nope, I am not going in that direction.

After dinner we necked. When was the last time you heard that term: "necked"? It was all so comforting, really, to be held in someone's arms and kissed while my laptop played classical music from the dinning room. But, let's face it, Nick was interested in more. (Heck, so was I!). I did my best to keep it at bay and not allow it a step further than kissing. Oh, yes I did! There is something wonderful just about kissing; it is the value of time together, without goals, to just enjoy each other. He wasn't all too simpatico with my thinking. But, ladies, don't apologize. If you have reservations about having sex with someone follow that inclination. If you are not ready, he just has to wait. I did try to explain that to him. I was unsure if he understood.

In conversation I had asked him what he wanted out of his life, what the time frame was. What were the possibilities he was offering. "We can either go in one of two directions: we can either have a wonderful time while you are here, knowing you will leave in a couple of months, or, we can possibly build on that, become closer and who knows what?" What I was hearing was anything was possible including a long-term committed relationship (but that conversation took place before I turned him down). He would have to fall in love with me; I was a good catch, hell, a fabulous woman (that is the Aries in me speaking)! I felt we were connecting, that we were similar with our expectations and hopes. Wrong. My thinking was inaccurate again. I was screwing up the whole thing by even considering l-o-v-e. Why do we women do that, anyway?

So night-night to Nick, celibate still (him, not I)... I still had Jules. Did I really need him to add to the complexities of my life? It was something I had to consider.

Apparently, he had his misgivings as disguised as they were. The next morning he sent me a note that implied, in a very round about way, that perhaps we were not a match and that he wanted different things than I did. Nothing like saying "No" to a man, huh? Men and women communicate so differently. We think differently, too. I suggested he wasn't giving "us" a full chance, and that he needed to practice a little patience and he might well have all-and more-he needed. The emails went back and forth and he set up a time to take me to the movies. But, I could tell his heart was no longer in it. That discouraged me, as well.

We had a glass of wine and a desert crepe together before the movie. It felt strained, but after all, the man works. He could have been bringing his own issues to the table; it might have nothing to do with me. I tried to breathe. We saw "Inglorious Bastards", which was one of the worst movies I have ever seen. Quentin Tarantino will not see me supporting his piggy bank in the future. The best part of the evening was his gently touching my hand throughout the movie. Other than that it was as much a bust of a night as our dinner date was fantastic. He kissed me lightly goodbye and I felt it: his spirit had moved away. His aura no longer intermingled with mine. Not a good sign. My Rhett Butler was gone, gone with the wind!

I had invited him over for dinner when my sister was visiting but he had declined. That in itself was interesting. He didn't want to be scrutinized by my sister. He would have been, for sure, but it wasn't like she would interrogate him. What a difference between he and Jules, who *wanted* to meet my sister. Perhaps, Nick's intentions were so dishonorable that he thought my sister would detect it and discourage me. She never had the chance to do that. He was doing it very well, himself.

I received another one of his emails that stated he thought I was "a sweet, gentle lady" but that it wasn't going to work. Huh? Mixed signals: how I detest men who don't know what the hell they want. But, if I am honest and kind here, I can say I think this actually showed a conscience. He thought I was more interested than he was and didn't want to break my heart down the road. I didn't know whether to be happy or sad. Mostly, I was disappointed. I could see myself long term with someone like Nick, but it wasn't reciprocal. So much for letting him see the longing of my heart.

We met one last time near Notre Dame for coffee at my request. The first thing he said to me was "I am not going to change my mind regardless of what you say." Ouch! What an ass! I laughed. I thought it was funny that his arrogance now permeated the conversation. We talked for fifteen minutes and I rather mocked him for the ambivalent garbage he put out there to me. Yes, he wanted a relationship. No he wasn't sure he wanted a relationship. Now, he allegedly wanted a French woman who lived close to him. Yes, someone sexy who didn't expect anything and would be classy and kind to his kids. Yada. Yada. Yada.

"Basically," I concluded to him "You are looking for a kind-hearted French vixen who lives in your backyard," I smirked. He recognized the irony of the well-worded summation. We women have heard this all before. Old news.

I was pleased that I had not bedded down with him. Had that been a good sexual experience for me I might have really been upset with his detour. I could have blessed him with my sacred inner sanctum. A privilege. Hell, an honor! Off, I huffed. Au revoir.

I didn't look back.

Fifteen

So, why the Eiffel Tower, you may wonder. Why not? I lived four blocks from the Eiffel Tower and it was an easy rendezvous for me. It was convenient. It also bustled with people morning, noon and night. In meeting someone for the first time it is of utmost importance to use your head and meet in a public place. Frankly, I thought if anyone stood me up I could easily walk home again. Thankfully, I was never stood up at least from a meeting scheduled for under The Eiffel Tower. It was a terribly romantic place. My second favorite place was Notre Dame but ND has a city-block wide court in front of it and it is often difficult to meet people you know, much less a stranger. One just gets enveloped in the crowd.

I love the energy of the Eiffel Tower. I have photographed some of its wonderful angles from a huge diversity of places, both near and far, day and night. It lends itself to photography. Even the illegal Nigerian hawkers, trying to sell their miniature Fiffel Towers, melt into the crazy energy of the scene. There were so many of them I am surprised the police didn't chase them off. Then there were the Afghanistan women who knew just enough English to ask you "Do you speak English?" Of course, the first time one asked me that I responded quickly and the woman hurried over to me to give me an index card written in English. It told me the story of her husband who allegedly was in a hospital in Afghanistan and would

I help with a donation. These women, usually young and fairly pretty, reported every morning to the Tower ready to solicit tourists. It was their job and they worked well into the evening; the Nigerians usually worked 'til the Tower closed at midnight. At first, both the Nigerians and Afghanistans were really annoying. When I considered, however, the drama of their lives and how they must live on the little they sold, my attitude changed. What individual stories they must have carried with them from their home countries to the Tower. Attitude changes everything, doesn't it? Then they meshed into the whole, hectic hodgepodge, intermingling with tourists from around the world and the craziness that always permeates from the Tower area. I developed a tolerance and appreciation for the whole crazy tornado of energy.

Meeting under the Tower seemed fairly easy. The center is the center is the center. Very little chance of missing your date. Add endless people and the watching ops were fascinating so if he was late, no problem. When we met, if I was not sure of him, I could suggest we just walk around the park and talk. Mostly, however, we went for a drink in a nearby café. Still public. Still safe.

Immediately south of the Tower is the Champs De Mars Park, which the military school, Ecole Militaire, used for training in a different era. Now it is divided into two massive grass areas, one of which is opened to the public normally for relaxing or picnicking.

Just to the north of the Tower is the Seine. Walking over the bridge towards Trocadero is a scenic walk, complete with a carousel for children, a playground, dancing water fountains and grass on which to relax. Walk up the steps of the curved palace colonnade framing the Trocadero and there are opportunities for impressive views and photos of the Tower. The energy and excitement is palpable.

At night, oh yes, and at night: The Eiffel Tower lights up at nighttime. Some times two thirds of the bottom would be red and the top white. Other times it would be blue and green. Apparently, they changed the colors to coordinate with sports events, international conferences, etc. It was cool; I never knew what to expect. And then, at the stroke of the hour it would sparkle like diamonds for five minutes. Usually, tourists were surprised. You could hear the collective "ahhh" and "Ohhhh" coming from the delighted crowds. Stay past those five minutes and you get a fifteen-minute light show with the colors of the Tower changing and moving constantly in patterns. Often I walked over in the daytime and exercised around the Tower and Champs de Mars along with other joggers and walkers. At night I would meander over, sometimes buy a chocolate crepe and just let the scene engulf me.

When my sister visited me, we huffed and puffed our way up the 720 stairs to level two, stopping to take photos of each other in the very heart of the Tower. In winter, they sometimes have a skating rink on the first level. Can you imagine: skating on the Eiffel Tower!

In September, as I have previously mentioned, along with twenty thousand other competitors from around the world I participated in that race from the Eiffel Tower to Versailles, some eighteen kilometers away. It was always exciting. It never got old; I never tired of any of it. And it was my good luck charm for meeting decent men. *And I lived four blocks away!*

Nick told me many people, particularly women, thought of it as a giant phallic symbol. I dismissed his crude inference, thinking how much they missed. The Eiffel Tower is a strong, huge structure but it has grace, strength, beauty and is rich in modern history. It is a beacon, a lure to the people of the world: Bienvenue a Paris! (*"Welcome to Paris!"*.) It is the beauty of the San Francisco Bridge, the Sydney Opera House, the Roman Forum, Big Ben in London, Victoria Falls, Africa or the Pyramids in Egypt combined into one, calling card to world tourists to come visit. And they do. It is *the most* visited monument in the modern world. More than 250 million people are estimated to have seen the Tower. Every morning, noon and night of every day of the year, rain, snow or fog, pilgrims from around the globe traipse over to gaze.

It bugged me…that sexual reference to the Tower. It underestimated the Tower. If sexual reference were not crude and inaccurate in itself take into consideration that when we refer to the Tower it takes on a *feminine gender,* not masculine. So thumbs down to all those awful people who want to sexualize my tower. My Eiffel Tower never failed to please. Can the men in my life ever compare to such an idea? Well, you know the answer to that.

But there was, oh brother was there, more to my life than that...

Sixteen

Ever since my American friend, Wade, told me about Hammams, I wanted to go. I love new experiences and embrace cultural differences. As Jules and I continued on with our relationship, he asked me to go to a couples' day at a Hammam someone recommended to him. Without hesitation I jumped at it. Off we went to Montmartre. *Montmartre*: that should have been a warning in itself.

First a disclaimer. Montmartre is the home to many respectable people with elegant and pricy homes. I know friends who live there and love it. It is the home to the white-faced hilltop basilica, Sacre Coeur, and other historic places. Long before it was incorporated into the city of Paris it grew vineyards on its hills and was home to many famous artists who roamed its streets, hopped its bars, hoping to sell a freshly painted canvas for the price of a drink.

But there is a seedier face to this area, as well. Prostitutes, drug dealers, you name it and it can probably be found in Montmartre. Pig Alley (Pigalle) offers sex shops, live sex shows, bars and any type of opportunity you may be seeking or not seeking.

But we were doing this in the daytime. I thought we would be fine. Think again.

It was actually cheaper for a couple on Couple's Day than for a single man to go in there on a general day. I suppose that was their way of discouraging perverts, or at least *impoverished* perverts. Women pay twelve euros; men, seventy-five, couples forty-eight combined. For Jules, who had allegedly never been there before, it was a deal!

As soon as we registered and paid the entrance I was questioning Jules with such innocent statements as "I don't know, Jules. I don't think this is a Hammam!" I whispered as we made our way to the locker room as we had been directed. He was given a towel and I a pareo. We changed in the co-ed locker room, where I noted another naked couple doing the same. Again, I looked at him quizzically. Again, he shook his head and told me not to worry. Hmmm.

There were only a few people when we arrived. We went into the steam room, having taken off our towel and pareo and sat down on our towels. No sooner did we settle in than a decrepit, weathered, old woman entered, naked as a jaybird, sat down directly next to me, our skin almost touching. Quickly, I looked over to Jules. "Don't worry" he seemed to nod to me, reassuringly and we stayed where we were. Now, what was this woman who could have sat anywhere in this large steam room, right next to *me* for? No sooner had I gotten that thought out than a shriveled, naked old guy opened the door and made his way over to the woman standing directly in front of her, his knee almost touching my knee. He lifted his soft manhood to her. *Shit! Why me, God?* With raised eyebrows and a shocked look, I glanced quickly at

Jules and he agreed, jumped up and escorted me out to the sauna, which was empty, thank goodness.

But the sauna had a huge picture window with rows of chairs facing it from the outside. Guess who followed us? Yep, the old fogies from the steam room. Apparently, they had taken a liking to us. They sat outside the sauna facing us, hoping for some action, I guess. It unnerved me.

"What are they staring at *us* for?" I asked. Jules shrugged. Clearly, this "charming" couple wanted to make our acquaintance. Clearly, we were not interested. Go away! Go away, I wanted to yell. They were annoying. Still, they were a couple that had probably been together a combined one hundred and fifty years and were still trying to keep their sex lives active. It was admirable in a way, I laughed later to Jules. But they were going to have to keep their love life exciting with someone else, not us. Secretly, I wondered, if this is what a girl has to do *forever* to keep her love life alive? I imagined myself in twenty years with my new young lover, sagging skin, boobs down to my navel, wrinkles and all, and hoped not. Maybe I would die young. Opps, too late!

More couples continued to arrive throughout the afternoon.

We went to the Jacuzzi. Here, one has to go in naked, so taking a deep breath, off my pareo came and in I climbed into the Jacuzzi hoping no one would notice my obvious flaws, just my svelte, slender body. The Jacuzzi was different than the steam room and sauna. The added dimension of bubbly water in which each couple was submersed was rather a turn on, I must admit. Not being able to see the entire body but, indeed, the blurred motions of their intertwining was sexy to me.

Now, I am not a prude. Really. I have seen pornography that elicited a reaction and served a purpose. But, generally, I think it far sexier to leave a little to the imagination. Later, I asked Jules, "If I could have taken a photo of something that afternoon, what do you think it would it have been?" "The Jacuzzi!" he laughed, without hesitation. It actually would have been the *sign* in French at the Jacuzzi which loosely translated to "No sexual contact". That was hysterical to me. I never actually saw anyone having sex in the Jacuzzi but it was sure a lot of foreplay going on there, heightened by those bubbles. God bless those bubbles; they sure did something for me. Eventually, we climbed out and went to have ourselves a glass of wine at the bar area. Really, at this point I could have used more than one.

As I slid through the Jacuzzi I accidentally brushed into the couple next to us, an attractive man and gorgeous woman who looked to be married, maybe even to each other. She smiled radiantly at me and I looked away, embarrassed and rushed off. As I emerged from the Jacuzzi, naked as the day I was created, she once again gave me a charming, lively smile. Hmmm.

Afterwards, as the place was filling up, we investigated the other areas of our "Hammam" more thoroughly. There was every conceivable type of room, most without locks, often with windows and opened doors to the hallway that beckoned the voyeur to come and watch or, perhaps, participate. My mouth gaped open. Couples were having sex right there in living color, so to speak. I was shocked and uncomfortable; Jules was enthralled. I sort of hid behind him while he and others watched with interest. Since this was my first and only visit to such a place I was, after all, a bit of a virgin…well, nearly. Everyone knew it was the first time there for both of us. When I peeked around him to see a couple, I whispered in his ear: "She is mort!" I was surprised to see a woman lying totally still with a man going down on her. She didn't lift a finger, a toe or flutter an eyelash. Her eyes were closed and her body was limp. Still, her partner had a go with her. How could anybody lie there *without reacting*? This went on for some time. I moved on. Boring!

Again and again, I found most couples unresponsive one to the other. Was oral sex and sexual intercourse so mundane? It would have turned me off to be putting myself out there for a lover who didn't respond. And sometimes it was the men, unresponsive, to a female. All I can say is my lovers had better respond or I am discouraged.

A Frenchman, who had just returned from New York that morning, started to talk to me about America. All I could think of was it didn't take him long to get to his "Hammam" upon his return. His partner, an Asian lady, was quiet and spoke no English. He asked me if I wanted to "play". I will never forget that. *"Play"*? What the hell did that mean: go outside and play on the swings? Ping-Pong, anybody? He saw the quizzical look on my face and assured me it was *only* "touching" that he wanted to do. *Touching*?

"Jules" I raised my voice just enough to get my lover's attention. "Come here!" My ever-protective, knight-in-shinning armor, Jules, took one look at me and the man standing with me and jumped to my side, and immediately retorted "No!" Later, he told me he didn't know what he was saying no to but that the expression on my astonished face told him all he needed to know. I exhaled.

Just about then, the good-looking couple, the man and dazzling woman from the Jacuzzi appeared in front of us and began speaking with Jules. As they spoke in French the woman lightly touched my arm in a friendly but somehow intimate gesture. I thought she wanted to "play". So did Jules. I didn't realize till much later that she had done the same flirtatious thing to Jules. He bit at it, of course, the young darlin'. But this woman's partner wanted private time with her immediately and one of the only private (lockable) rooms was available so he hurried her away. Jules and I stood there. What was that all about?

I have never had a "female" experience. I don't really think I am gay or bisexual. Still, I think many women have a curiosity about what intimacy with another woman would be like. Would it be provocative, stimulating? How would it affect my relationship with Jules (or he with me)? Did she want a threesome, a partner exchange or what? Would I be embarrassed? Would I barf? Worse than that, what if I actually liked it? The fact that I didn't speak much French was a hindrance, for sure. I didn't know what they were saying. *I really had to learn more French!*

Jules wanted to stay longer and talk with them to "Make their acquaintance" as he put it. "Maybe" he stated in his thick French accent "we can get to know them outside of here". I was getting confused with it all and we had been there a long time. I was tired. Steam, Sauna, Jacuzzi, watching couples "play" was exhausting. Grandma needed a nap.

Fantasies sometimes need to remain fantasies. I do not regret not acting on this. This type of lifestyle, this type of experience was an affront to my middle-class ethnic upbringing. I was concerned about STDs, too. Who wouldn't be, although it seemed apparent everyone used condoms. If, indeed, it would have been enjoyable what would I do with that knowledge? How would it have affected my life? Perhaps, it would have been like caviar: you learned to like it. I wasn't at all sure I wanted to acquire that in my old age. Wasn't life complicated enough just dating men? I just wasn't up to the activities at that place and probably never would be.

I should state here this really was not a "Hammam". That is how Jules lured me there. This really was more a sex club than a Hammam. Down the road I would go to a real Hammam "Ladies" day and enjoy it with full spa options such as facials, body scrubs and the best massage I ever had. Hammams are expensive but a special treat every now and then. So I don't want any complaining Hammam owners to call me because dear Jules took me to a sex club, not a real Hammam.

For those of us who survived the 70s without exchanging house keys and partners (that would be me), without frequenting sex clubs (that would also be me), this was quite an experience. If truth be told, I always wondered how I would react. In watching these couples I found it all very forced, very phony. There were couples who were screwing and the women didn't seem to enjoy it at all. They were robots. Perhaps they were there trying to please their partners without really enjoying it. I did hear a few moans and groans coming from a couple of women but mostly it all seemed sort of …well…*unloving*, robotic. For me, it was uncomfortable. Yep, and other than the stimulating, bubbly Jacuzzi, it was boring, albeit a different kind of boring but boring, nonetheless. I would have preferred spending the afternoon in bed at home alone with Jules. "Toto, I want to go home" I thought to myself, kicking my feet together twice. Jules, however, seemed to thrive on watching.

I wasn't in Kansas, anymore.

Seventeen

Jules: our relationship continued in between my dates with other men. This wasn't always as easy to accomplish as it may seem. For most people, sex tends to bond you to another individual in a way that encourages monogamy. Jules and I became closer. That showed when he continued to ask me about the men I went out with.

"Are they kissing you?" he asked me quietly in bed one afternoon. "Are they touching you?" Clearly, it wasn't easy for him, either.

I attended Meet Up functions. There is nothing more attractive than a happy person. I glided through those social evenings with confidence and grace. I was alive, well and living in Paris, just like Jacques Brel. Why wouldn't I be happy? So Meet Ups became regularly scheduled functions. For those who are unacquainted with this, Meet Up is an international organization where you can register your interests, hobbies etc. Local Meet Up organizers will contact you with information about individual groups in your area. I joined a hiking group and found that quite enjoyable. I joined a social group and was content speaking my own language again. I joined a Night Life group but saw that most of the members were half my age and I didn't return. I joined a bunco group but attended only once. Too busy.

Out of one of the social groups came a charming English man who lived in Canada and visited his daughter in Paris twice a year. He was actually older than I am, an unusual occurrence, and one that I welcomed. His name was Trent. In his day, he must have been a really great looking guy because at his age (I am guessing about seventy) he was still a good-looking chap. He was a retired professor so there would be no fancy, culinary extravaganzas but still his wit and intelligence were attractive. He managed to find a charming little restaurant in my arrondissement and we enjoyed the evening together. He had a wonderful, dry British sense of humor.

When I told him I was writing a book about the men in my life, he quietly asked with his dry Brit humor "And will it be a *large* volume?"

Without missing a beat, I replied "Two".

We both took a sip of our wine.

Trent and I made a date to take the train to Chartres to see the town and cathedral. We were rained out. We met at the train station and decided at the last minute that we did not want to walk around in the rain in Chartres so off we went to a museum neither of us had been to before. Heck, I hadn't even heard of it before I checked with my travel guru, Rick Steves.

Marmottan Museum (Musee Marmottan Monet) is a little known, private home converted into a collection of works by Claude Monet. It is another opportunity to learn and appreciate Monet even more. And we did. With more than a hundred works of art from sketches of his early life to the well-known lily pods in his garden, it was a beautiful, relaxing tour through the mansion that showcased it so perfectly. The rain drizzled outside but inside our hearts, minds and souls were warm, cozy and content.

Trent came home with me; I had promised him dinner, which I had made ahead of time. Now, listen once you get into that tiny closet of an elevator it is almost impossible *not* to get kissed. So it wasn't a stretch – literally or figuratively – to find our lips meeting. He wasn't all over me like many of the French guys but the tenderness of the kiss is what got my attention. Men will never know how important that first kiss is and I am not going to elaborate on it here. There will be a whole chapter on kissing soon enough.

We enjoyed a lovely early meal and I bid him adieu as efficiently as I could. He managed to grab a kiss with much more, ah, how shall I say this….err, *emphasis* to it then the one on the elevator. The elevator kiss was better. Many older men kiss a bit old fashioned with tight, closed lips pressing hard against a woman's. It is not particularly passionate to me. A man simply must know how to kiss me if he is to maintain my interest. I had no time to teach him as he was leaving Paris a few days later. So tally ho, my dear Englishman. It was a pleasure to share Paris with you.

Then came my Buddhist buddy, Dikran, who contacted me through Craig's List, who wasn't particularly attractive from his photo but that didn't deter me. He sounded interesting, different and more spiritual than the men I knew in Paris, who were usually atheists, agnostics or non practicing Catholics (or two of the three). I needed a break. We met under the Eiffel Tower and then headed over to the fourth arrondissement, the Jewish quarters, where there were lots of interesting cafes, bistros, boutiques, gays and bars. The Marais is one of my favorite areas in Paris. After the French Revolution an architect, Baron Georges-Eugene Haussmann, was hired to blast away many of the smaller, quaint streets of Paris so potential revolutionaries could not hide from the army should there ever be another revolution. Haussmann was quite controversial in his day (and even today). Imagine! All the centuries-old streets destroyed mainly because of paranoia left over from the revolution a hundred years earlier. But Marais today has maintained many of its quaint, narrow streets because it wasn't slated to get demolished too early in the plan. Then World War I drew demolition crews and plans away from execution. It offers an authentic glimpse of what Paris was like pre-French Revolution. I have walked the streets there more than anywhere else. That is the neighborhood so many tourists now flock to visit or stay.

Dikron was a tall, bald man with black rim glasses. Lean from a healthy diet and no meat, he shared with me his Buddhist beliefs and we discussed spirituality and religiosity, both of which I found enormously interesting.

Apparently, he was trying to live in peace, love and *celibacy*.

"So, how's that celibacy thing workin' for you?" I smiled at him.

"At times, it is most trying" he sighed, brave, pure man that he was, managing his only smile of the night.

You betcha. Myself, I preferred smiling to celibacy.

Bye-bye, Dikron. Peace be with you.

Then there was Claude Pierre. Or, maybe I should say there almost was Claude Pierre. Claude Pierre was a Frenchman, an attorney, who spent a lot of time talking with me on the phone. It looked like he worked all the time (red flag) but, finally, we made a date to go out. He spoke great English, had lived in the U.S., had a good sense of humor and liked American women.

We agreed to meet at a metro stop in the sixth arrondissement near where he lived and worked. *Big mistake*. I should have required he meet me under the Eiffel Tower. Men should always come to *your* turf. Remember that. Before my stop came up, the police evacuated the metro I was in. Everybody out! Apparently, there was a bomb scare. In fact, some yoyo decided to call in a bomb threat to the metro authorities. Can you believe it? They evacuated several of the metros. Christ, what a girl has to go through to get a date!

When my sister and I spent our last evening together before her departure, we had such a great time I managed to actually break my toe and *not know I had* until several hours later. We had taken a pricey dinner cruise on the Seine. Her treat. The food was average at best but the wine flowed freely and relaxed us entirely. So, yeah, we got a little drunk. She was sure that the dove following our boat was "The Holy Spirit". Sure it was, Sis. We walked home from the dock near the Tower fully feeling the "spirits" we had consumed. OK, *I felt it*. I am not a big drinker and I would suffer the consequence of that. I exclaimed to my fellow Parisians, snug asleep in their boudoirs, "J'taime, Paris!" (OK, at the top of my voice at midnight). I am sure that endeared me to them. I felt great and I had not in any way yet suffered the effects of a broken toe along the path of our final night together. I would, however, and it would be a royal pain in the tush, as well as the foot.

So it came to be that I hobbled along on a broken toe to where I was supposed to meet good old Claude Pierre. I hadn't expected to walk much so I went along with the initial game plan sans any idea of the potentiality of an *evacuation*. I didn't have a cell phone or C-Pierre's number with me, either. *Mistake again.* So off I shuffled down the street to the metro stop where we were supposed to meet, more than a mile away. Down dark rues, up abandoned streets I limped till I found the darn metro stop. It was a hot, humid night. My feet were swelling, my toe aching, and my face sweating. What the hell did I put on make up for, I fumed.

Finally, after much ado I arrived at our agreed metro. Lo and behold, guess who wasn't there! Surprise! He had assumed I wasn't coming. Crap. To boot, I was hungry. There is something in my metabolism that craves good food that correlates to a good mood. An old boyfriend, Mel, used to say (and he was correct) my mood always improved when I was fed well. That was a fact. I am not a nutritionist or chemist but something happens to me when I am hungry which is totally opposite of how I feel when I dine well. Anyway, back to my little story.

Apparently, the French police take their bomb scares seriously. Several of the metros closed down. With few cabs in Paris and loads of metro passengers trying to hail them down, it took a long time to find a cab. I was on that street corner over an hour with every cab passing by, already filled with other frustrated metro passengers. This is what I get, I reasoned, for not meeting under the Eiffel Tower! I never did find a cab on my own; a kind cafe waiter whistled one over in three minutes after I finally asked for his help. Home I headed, pissed off that good old Claude Pierre might have given me the name and address of the restaurant, as I had requested originally, and I would have found him there. I couldn't be at fault for any of this, could I? Hmmm.

I eventually made it home. Frankly, I was irritated. I was tired, and hurting and hungry and out fifteen euros for the cab.

The phone was ringing as I entered my apartment. It was Claude Pierre acting concerned about what happened. But, he didn't want to come over to my arrondissement and pick me up and take me out. He didn't offer to pay for the cab, either. Didn't he get it? He would have been out with the Queen of Craig's List, for God's sake! Where was the respect? Scratch that guy. I dropped him like a hot potato. His loss. A lesson learned. God's will be done.

Still, most of the men I met were acceptable, some even better than that and a few of them were married. But the truth is that the married men and I got along great and most of them, business men, just wanted to have a pleasant evening out with a decent woman, nothing more. If they harbored "impure" thoughts, as the Catholics would say, they always stayed gentlemen.

So, dating in Paris can be as exasperating as dating in Detroit or Tallahassee, just different scenery and different accents.

Still, the platonic dates were sometimes worth it. I met George, an American, through Craig's List (Maybe I should send a Thank You note to Craig's List! What would I have done without them?) George was a really pleasant guy who invited me to lunch but then expected me to pay. Horrors! When a man expects me to pay he waives all chances of romance. How can a girl get romantic with a man who doesn't have enough money, interest or willingness to pay for lunch? OK, so I guess a little of the Cinderella Complex was rearing its ugly head. I never said I was perfect.

Women of "a certain age" were indoctrinated with the idea of a man taking care of them. Younger women tend not to have that same complex. Because of the sixties generation those same younger women can now claim more employment opportunities with, if not equal pay, closer to equal pay than we women of the sixties. Without equal pay there is no equality in the relationship. For me, because I was married only once to someone who did not want me to work outside of the home I clung to that belief system. If a man is the bread earner or makes more, he pays. I could and did repay him with lovely home cooked dinners, which I always did to express my appreciation. I never had a boyfriend who didn't think I gave a great amount in the relationship. Older men love that *anyone* would be willing to cook for them. They tell me career women never want to enter the kitchen. Whatever happened to the idea that a man should woo a woman, should "court" her in a sense. Gone with the ERA!

I knew right away this date would go nowhere. But I liked him nonetheless. We had similar interests in travel, history, and stained glass. We walked a lot that day all over the place just enjoying whatever we happened upon. We made a date to go to the Cluny Museum, which he loved. I had not been there yet but I was game. Off we went. The Cluny is such a delightful surprise. All those endless, exquisite stained glass windows that I had been admiring at all the cathedrals, were so high and far away from eye level one needed binoculars to fully appreciate the intricate detail. But not here. Not at the Cluny which displayed stained glass portions from Sainte Chappelle and other gothic buildings right there *on eye level*. You could shoot away at them and I photographed every single one of them in every room. The photos came out great because they were lit up from behind. I loved the Cluny. We ended up in the Latin Quarter going for hot chocolate. Dutch, of course.

I told him about all the free music concerts in Paris and suggested he and his buddy join me for one. They both took me up on it. But first, I told him about my next apartment, which I loved but had reservations about the neighborhood in the nineteenth. George promised to walk all the way there (another great walker) and scout it out during the next day. He suggested he and his buddy and I would go after the concert at nighttime and check it out. I was, of course, most grateful for the thoughtfulness and told him so. The neighborhood, while not as charming as the area around the Eiffel Tower by any stretch, appeared safe. We went for wine and then took the metro back to central Paris, where we bid each other adieu since George was leaving soon thereafter. That type of "date" is perfectly acceptable. They don't all have to be candidates for Romance of the Century. It was worthwhile to pass the time with a good person.

Being a woman in Paris can be an intoxicating experience. I splurged on a ticket to my favorite Opera house, Opera Garnier. I donned my best black, sexy, little cocktail dress, full makeup, high heels, hell, even nylons and off I hastened, attitude and all. Opera Garnier is the most decadent, opulent, gorgeous opera house I have ever visited anywhere in the world, and I have been all over Mother Earth. If ever you are going to dress up this would be the place. And, while there were many who dressed to the hilt, still others wore jeans. Can you imagine? The gay couple sitting next to me had on jeans. I wanted to shake them. "You are at the most beautiful Opera house in the world, for God's sake, straighten up!" But I kept my demure presence and composure under control.

At intermission, I rose slowly from my orchestra seat, head held high, shoulders back, tummy tucked in as much as possible and promenaded through the exquisite structure like I owned it. People gawked. Yes, they did! Oh, the power! I slowly sauntered passed two men who stopped in mid conversation to fully appreciate the woman (that would be me) walking by them. I was sixty-three years old and still turning heads. There is a God.

Eighteen

I consider myself a woman's woman. Women need to be faithful allies to other women; they need to listen to each other's problems, feel each other's pain and vow we should never go out of our way to hurt a fellow sister-woman. I pretty well observe that in my daily life. Forget those married guys who come on to you while they are sitting next to their wives. Screw 'em. Or better yet, *don't!*

Still, I found that dining with married men in Paris was often a load of fun. But I would find out that not all married men are innocent in their intentions.

I can't forget Sonny. Sonny was a Nuclear Physicist. Sonny found me under "platonic" on Craig's List and was coming in from Denver to attend a conference in Geneva. We met at the Eiffel Tower and walked over and had a glass of wine together in early afternoon.

We had pre-arranged to dine together that evening. He, like most married men in Paris, told me about his marriage. It always amazes me how many people are unhappily married. He was no different but felt it was too expensive to divorce. Excuses, excuses. Anyway, later that evening, when he was running late he called and asked me to take a cab to his hotel and they would recommend a restaurant for us in the area. I did that and he was waiting outside to pay the cab driver and bless him for that. We walked a block from the east end of the Louvre and had a lovely meal and lively conversation in a nearby bistro. It eventually became evident that Sonny was hoping for more than I was willing to consider. Even though originally he had wanted to go out to a nightclub afterwards, when he arrived at the conclusion that I was not going to sleep with him, he lost interest. Fine. No problem. He gave me the cabbie money and off I was whisked home, "virtue" still intact, not having misrepresented myself (I had listed under *platonic*, if you recall) and content with the majority of the evening, conversation and meal.

Jan, an American lawyer in Chicago, my hometown, communicated with me regularly prior to getting to Paris. He, too, was married. He made it clear ahead of time he did not want any romance, just a companion with whom to experience Paris. He liked the idea that I lived in Paris and assumed I would know my way around. That was fine; I knew my way around more than he did, that is for sure, but I was still hobbling around on my broken toe. Not wanting to disappoint him, however, I shuffled over to his hotel to meet him for a day of discovering Paris. We stumbled upon a Tiffany exhibit at the Luxembourg Palais. We both enormously enjoyed that exhibit and it was clearly more fun to share it with a companion. As the storm clouds gathered, off we hurried to a well-known eatery in the sixth arrondissement, Brasserie Le Lipp near the eglise St Germaine des Pres. My foot was in agony, by now, after too much walking.

We arrived at a typical, packed restaurant with waiters running like French hens with their heads cut off. Zip! No time for charm! Zap! No time for smiles. They eventually escorted us upstairs, also packed, but slightly quieter and we settled into our table, happy to be out of the rain. There is something wonderful about the rain in Paris. In the matter of a few minutes the rain went from a single droplet to a crashing thunderstorm and thirty minutes beyond that the drama abruptly ended. The symbolism of the passion of Paris did not elude me. It was all marvelous as we sat there with our wine. Service was slow as is the tradition of Paris cafes but we were safe, dry and cozy inside.

Eventually, our lunch came, and through our candid conversation, Jan and I shared some of the details of our lives. He was a fifty-year old attorney, still married with two children at home. He and his wife slept in different rooms and were barely on speaking terms. But he definitely was not looking to me for anything beyond sharing Paris for a day. He was a good guy, a good-looking one to boot. He had a solid moral compass and I have to say I felt sorry that such a good man was stuck in an unloving relationship, at least for the time.

Children bind these men to the women, and often vice versa. They are all allegedly waiting for their children to grow up so they can separate. I am not at all convinced that is the best thing to do but these married gents I met thought it was. They were willing to make the sacrifice of their own personal lives for their children. Probably, their wives were making the same sacrifice.

We had a wonderful day in Paris and finally I grabbed a metro home with plans to meet Jan for dinner a couple of hours later. Originally, in communication with me before he left the States, Jan told me to make a reservation at a good restaurant. Never say that to a "foodie" in Paris! I checked my restaurant books for haute cuisine and went on line to make a reservation. I found several two and three-star restaurants, but, oddly, they were closed on Saturday and Sunday. By the time I found one to take my reservations, I grabbed at the opportunity. They were confirmed reservations at a two-star restaurant! I was thrilled! Then I went on line to look at their menu. I was stunned. If Jan had taken me there for dinner it would have cost him about $1,000.00! Hey, I was a good "date" but *a $1,000 for dinner*? I don't think so!

So I turned to Jules, my dear Jules. Jules often recommended restaurants for my dates and me. I know. Odd, isn't it? Anyway, he made restaurant reservations at Le Dome on boulevard du Montparnesse, next to Le Coupole, for Jan and me. Again, Jules was right on the mark. It was an elegant, lovely restaurant but didn't require a man to have to sell two of his children to pay the bill. We both were in great moods; it had been a lovely day. Jan encouraged me to order anything I wanted. God bless him. We started off with a lobster salad, a whopping fifty-seven euros ($90 US) and split it. It was good, but *ninety bucks*? Jan had some money, I was sure, but still it was a generous gesture and one I appreciated to no end.

Next we each ordered a succulent, perfectly cooked veal chop, which was fabulous. Swallowing down a wine Jan personally knew and thought was a "deal" (a deal in Paris?) priced at a hundred euros (@$150 at that time) was delightful. It slid down my throat real easily, I can tell you that.

Then we splurged on dessert (like we weren't "splurging" before?) We split a humongous piece of cake that was out of this world and enough to feed a family of four. My metabolism was singing! I was delighted and excited at such a wonderful experience. Somehow, miraculously, I wasn't feeling the pain in my toe any more.

We hopped in a cab and took off for the jazz club I had suggested, Le Caveau De La Huchette in the Latin Quarter. It is a well-known dance place and one needs to walk down cave-like steps to the basement where the live music and dancing awaited. It was just what we each hoped it would be: very Parisian. There were regulars customers on the dance floor who could have won a professional competition like "Dancing with the Stars". Heck, now that I think about it, many of them might have been pros. They sure were terrific at dancing.

Jan didn't want to dance and I could hardly blame him. It was daunting watching such talented dancers. But I was tortured. My toe was beginning to hurt again, but oh, how I wanted to dance. I pride myself on my ability on the dance floor. So, off I went, with Jan's blessing, and asked one of the older guys to dance. He was wonderfully energetic and talented and it took all my concentration to keep up with him but my toe told me this would be the only dance for me that evening.

It was two-thirty in the morning when we found our way out of our cave. We had had a perfect day in Paris. Just pure fun. Then, we turned to getting a cab.

Anyone who knows anything knows that the metros stop basically at midnight. Cabs must be called on the phone. There are few enough around, any way. We queued up in line for about thirty minutes with twenty people in front of us. Not one cab arrived. So off we walked to find a cab. And we walked and we walked and we walked, broken toe and all. Honestly, had I not had a toe issue and had my sneakers on I could have walked home but this was now 3:00 am and we hadn't a clear idea of how to get a taxi.

Eventually, Jan practically threw himself in front of a stopped, empty cab that was off-duty and begged him to take us home. I'll never forget that cab driver. What a nice guy! First, we dropped off Jan at his hotel, which was closer and then I went on home. Jan offered the driver a fifteen-euro tip, way over what most people paid. Unbelievably, the driver handed back ten euros to him saying five was enough. Can you imagine? *A French cab driver with a conscience*?!

I arrived home around four in the morning, happy, content and pleased with the whole day and evening. My adrenaline was still pumping (another N.O. high) and I had a hard time falling asleep.

Perhaps, I was lucky. Perhaps, I didn't give these married men a "vibe". Perhaps, I screened them properly beforehand but I had these types of experiences more than once. There are businessmen passing through Paris who legitimately don't want to spend an evening eating alone at a restaurant. Neither do I. That is why I went out with them. No ulterior motives.

Another wonderful date was Nelson. Nelson was a Frenchman living in the States. He flew to France frequently on business. He had begun his business from scratch. Now his company was selling to major accounts like Wal-Mart and Costco. He had been married for decades, and he didn't really want to talk about it. That was fine; neither did I.

Again, through Craig's List, I had corresponded with Nelson prior to his Paris arrival. We had exchanged photos, as well. I don't know what it is about men but they sure don't give a second thought to the quality of their photographs. I have never met a man whose photo did him justice. But, of course, there is so much more to it than looks, anyway: presence, style, personality, intelligence, sophistication are not always apparent in those awful photos they sent.

When I told Jules that Nelson was coming in he recommended two restaurants to me and then took me to look at them and the menus. I chose Chez Francis, which had a direct view of my dear, beloved Eiffel Tower. One can dress in jeans for the outdoor café area, but indoor was dressier, which was fine with me. I waited and then took a window table that had been reserved for me. Unbeknownst to me, Nelson had arrived through a different door and was sitting elsewhere in the restaurant waiting for me. A half hour went by. I was hungry. My metabolism was fading. I checked with the maitre d', with the hostess and no man had arrived asking for me. I checked the bar. No solo men. Back to my table. I ordered a drink. I had full makeup on (yep, even mascara) and was dressed to the hilt. I thought I might as well order a drink even if he is a no show. Unbeknownst to me,

Nelson was doing the same thing in a different part of the restaurant.

Eventually, the maitre d' figured it out, escorted him to my table, apologized and offered to buy us our drinks. Nelson was better looking than his picture. He was well dressed, moxy and I liked him immediately. The fact that he ordered a bottle of Rodier Champagne had absolutely nothing to do with it. Ummm! "We must start with oysters!" he declared and so we did. The food was excellent, the wait staff was now bending over backwards trying to make up their faux pas, the view of the Tower enchanting. Nelson, sweet Nelson, had brought me a little gift, a French cookbook, because he knew I liked to cook. It was, blessedly, in Anglais.

When dinner was over we decided to walk to the Eiffel Tower. There he bought me a rose and we watched the lights go out at midnight. It was one of my most charming dates in Paris and I was grateful for every moment. We hopped in a cab and I was home in five minutes, giving him a quick peck on the check before I jumped out at my doorstep. I hope our paths cross again. I have a feeling they will.

"Dating" married men in Paris was different, however, than at home. I would never get socially or romantically linked to a married man in my area. It is the path of self-destruction. But, in Paris, in the beauty of the 'City of Lights" I relaxed my usual rules and with no expectation of anything beyond the moment, enjoyed Paris with them.

Another married man (but he didn't tell me so, initially) was Luke. Luke and I rendezvoused under the Eiffel Tower. He was a good-looking man, about fifty, and we decided to dine walking distance in Trocadero. We strolled up to the restaurant L'Homme from the nearby Tower. It was a cozy restaurant, slow again in service but we patiently sipped our bottle of Veuve Clicquot Champagne and talked. He resided in Paris and was separated from his wife, who lived in another city. Still, he did not hesitate to tell me he was looking for more than a friend.

After dinner, we walked back to the Eiffel Tower. Then he walked me home, we said goodnight and up I went to my apartment alone, like the good little girl I am. I would see him again. Still, I began to ask myself if I was I playing with fire here?

American-born Ben ran his ad on Craig's List, as well, and one of us found the other. I met him for lunch in the thirteenth at a typical, little Parisian café complete with red checked table clothes. I think Ben was in his late forties, married with two kids, one still in the nest. He told me that his wife had been asking him for a divorce for three years, but that he wanted to get the last little one, now sixteen, out of the nest before granting his spouse her wish.

This, allegedly, was his first ad on Craig's List. He just wanted to see what was out there and how he felt in the dating scene. We became good friends, nothing more, although he was attractive enough to have been considered for the coveted title as "The lover of the Queen of Craig's List". Still, we meet every couple of weeks for a couple of drinks and to talk. I hope to see him again because I consider him a friend.

Occasionally, just to surprise me, I'd find a man under platonic who actually wanted only a "cultural exchange" and nothing more. Jean Claude and I met a few times to help each other with language development. He, I thought, was actually excellent in English, far better than I was in French so I may have benefited more than he. He was an honest young man probably not yet 40. He always showed up in a business suit at some café and he sincerely wanted to perfect his English. There appeared to be many people who wanted to move to the States. Jean Claude wanted to move his family there. When I asked him if his wife knew he was meeting with me he responded "Oui!" and I knew he was a decent guy.

I am not advocating that women should date married men but if you are really careful (of your life as well as your heart) and keep your feet firmly grounded without an emotional attachment, meeting for a tour or dinner can be fun while out of your hometown. It certainly introduced me to some delicious restaurants! But sexual involvement was not my goal. After all, I had Jules.

Nineteen

It might seem strange to you that in the midst of my sexual memoirs lies the longest chapter in the book and that it is on *kissing*. That is because long after your ability and interest in sex wanes the pleasure of pure (and impure kissing) remains tantamount to the quality of your life. From birth, when we get that first maternal kiss on the forehead, to our death bed when loved ones step up to say their final adieu, kissing adds a dimension to our lives that cannot be disputed.

But, does *anyone* ever get enough kissing? Do *you* get kissed enough?

Kissing is the gateway "drug". Even the Chinese knew this long ago: "Kissing is like drinking salted water. You drink and your thirst increases." Kissing opens us up, nay, *encourages* us to take it a step further, further, further till we loose sight of its true, pure value and just hurry to the goal: sex. What a shame! What a crime! American men, correction, *most* men everywhere are too "goal-oriented". The only goal, if you must have one, is to enjoy the journey, not arrive at the destination.

Do you remember the first kiss you had? I bet you do. I do. After all these decades, I still know his name and remember the whole scenario. Lenny Jensen and I attended the last two years of grammar school together. We were thirteen and he was about to move away. He told me later he had an older brother who strongly advised him on the eve of the move, to claim that first kiss before it was too late. Over he trod from his house to mine that lovely summer evening.

In our Chicago neighborhood we all had stoops and families often would hang out in the summer evenings talking. Teenagers would wait till their parents went indoors and then hung out with their friends. At thirteen I had never been kissed before. I sensed Lenny was nervous; I thought it was about the move. It was not; it was about me, us, err…the kiss! Finally, after hemming and hawing for some time, he told me the truth: he wanted to kiss me. I, at thirteen, felt my heart beating wildly but I didn't want him to know that. I waited till he made the first gesture. Eventually, with my eager anticipation (and implied consent), he placed a five second kiss square on my lips. Then he looked down, exhaled loudly, clearly ready to faint.

Me? I pretended that we did this every day. I was cool, you see; I didn't want him to know how exciting this all was for me. I could hardly process it myself.

Then, he said with renewed courage "One more" and I received my second kiss. I was thrilled, he relieved. Relieved enough to get up and say he had to go home. After all, we both needed to think about what we had just experienced. But, the truth was, I *wanted* to ask him to stay.

I Goggled the topic of kissing and found a quote from Leonard Di Caprio about his first kiss. "The first kiss I had was the most disgusting thing in my life. The girl injected a pound of saliva into my mouth and when I walked away I had to spit it all out!" Yuck. She nearly ruined it for the future lucky women in young Leo's life; how discouraging a kiss can be! My educated guess, however, is that Leo's kisses vastly improved with better partners.

Still I, too, have endured many official members of the Kissing Hall of Shame: A would-be suitor I had known a few years came over to visit and finally got around to kissing me. His kisses were so wet I felt like I should get on a wet suit I refer to him as The Fish Kisser. Were we snorkeling here? I don't see any beach! When men or women slobber so much salvia around your mouth that the skin outside your mouth and chin actually gets chapped it is NOT fun. It is NOT passionate. Unless, of course, you are taking a medicine that actually dries your mouth out, it serves no useful function. Not surprisingly, he never did become a lover of mine.

That reminds me of a lover I did have more than a decade ago: Rob (The Drooler). Right in the middle of lovemaking he actually drooled on me. I might as well have gone to bed with the puppy. That was it. Good-bye! So long! Au revoir! Arrivederci! Auf Wiedersehen! Sayonara! *Drool?* Gross. Curses to the person who bestows sloppy kisses!

Why is a kiss so important? For two thirteen-year olds, it was the first sign of maturity. But it was the awakening of something we had not yet experienced, the connection of two people in one, the intimacy of crossing over that bridge from friendship to more. It was surrender at its most innocent form. It was the acknowledgement that I was a girl and he was a boy.

Idyllically, we lose ourselves and hand our spirit over to another being and they to us. It is the sweet abandonment of the world. The reason we close our eyes, after all, is to shut out the world. Then we step into each other's space, literally and figuratively, intermingling our auras in an almost spiritual way. Yes, *spiritual*. Two people are becoming one. They are being what God created them to be. Have you ever heard the saying: "We are spiritual beings having a human experience"? Many of us believe it is true. During a kiss, the world becomes invisible. We twirl around in a space created just for our partner and our self. We are in our own little universe and with a good kiss, you are each the center of that universe. What could be better? Anyway, *that is the way it is meant to be*, but sadly, few understand kissing on that profound level.

But, let's face it; *a whole lot of kissing is happening the world-over that isn't associated with love*. Do we then accept the lowest common denominator in kissing? Do we kiss less? Do we spend little time on *creative* kissing? Do we hurry forward? Do we underestimate its importance? Too many would answer "oui" to any one of those questions!

I can count on one hand how many men in my entire life truly knew how to kiss and who appreciated its value. I can still remember each and every one of them. Most kissers are Functional Kissers (FKs). Experience helps and most can turn someone on but the lingering, the true nurturing that a good kiss, a loving kiss, gives is often lost on the masses. For most, kissing serves merely as the escalator to something more. Basically, it is a quick segue to lovemaking. The keynote word of that last sentence: *quick*. When a lover spends all of three minutes kissing you before intercourse, you both miss enormous pleasures. Usually, at the beginning of a relationship, a man goes out of his way to seduce a woman with lengthy kissing. Then, after the successful seduction, oftentimes doesn't feel he needs to bother with this step at all any more. Let's get to the point, he implies, as he hurries past a few kisses, onward to sex. Now, look, maybe sometimes you both want to do it that way. I get it. Just don't make it a habit to rush. *Make it a habit not to rush*. News Flash*: It is not a crime to kiss*! You are, after all, raising your Nitric Oxide!

I remember one of my lovers, Rob (you remember The Drooler), who was taking Viagra, which apparently promised a forty-minute wait before beginning its magical spell, approach me with a question. Rob asked me about a new, recently released competitor to Viagra that could work in five minutes. Would I like him to take that, instead? Are you kidding me? I sighed. He was missing the idea. "No" I replied. "I want the time with you. I don't want to hurry forward passed all the good stuff." He got it. Or at least I think he got it. He never mentioned it again.

Frankly, I recommend to all couples, to devote one day or evening weekly to kissing *only*. Make a pact: *no sex* (that idea in itself becomes a turn on). Pretend, if you must, you are both teenagers and your parents are soon to return home. *No sex*! Then sit back and look, really look at each other. Practice a variety of kissing. Rediscover each other. But, *No sex!*

Let's switch back to the Functional Kissers of the world; the majority of kissers are FKs, as I previously stated. Let's face it, even if our partner is not attuned to a higher level of kissing they still are able to turn us on and we are grateful for something, which is better than nothing, after all (*but, oh, that it would be more!*). I remember going to lunch with "the girls", if you can call us grannies, girls (you can in my case!). I was telling them about the first date I had recently had with some guy and that he kissed me at the end. One girlfriend, fully forty years into her marriage, was shocked. "You let him kiss you on the first date?!" (Not everyone is with the agenda, kids). I laughed, "*Let* him kiss me? Hell, I nearly *thanked* him!" (It had been a long time since I had been kissed.)

We are talking about the quality of life here, folks. We human beings need nurturing, damn it!

Back to terra firma: If you *don't* like the way someone kisses you, what do you do? Well, I can tell you that truth must be balanced with *tact*. It is the only way to go. I know. I never tried that route! All too many times, I found it easier to just not see the guy again rather than trying to teach him how I wanted to be kissed (or anything else). Men have egos the size of Wyoming, anyway. So, in that vein, in my effort to *not* offend the man I was with, I would get through the kiss and just never see him again. "*Get through*"? No one should lose out on what might be a meaningful relationship because step one (kissing) is gross.

There was this very sweet man who cheerfully came over to my house to help with some home problem (every woman should have such a friend). But we had had a few dates with a perfunctory kiss at the end of the night. Nothing heart-melting. This time, as he left I tried to encourage something more. Be careful of what you wish for.

When he caught on to the idea of my interest in more than an ordinary peck, he went wild. He grabbed me, jammed his tongue down my throat and wouldn't let go. I tried to breathe but couldn't. Gasping, I tried to indicate "enough". His tongue was like a propeller in my mouth (I call him the Propeller Kisser.). And this kamikaze pilot was about to kill me with that propeller. *SOS! Stop!* For God's sake, I was being choked, strangled really to death by his slimy, long tongue! The more I gasped for air the more he misinterpreted the gasping as passion and forged onward and inward. I thought his tongue was trying to reach my intestines. What the hell? Was he giving me a colonoscopy? Needless to say I didn't see him again. *It was way, way too much.* And it was gross. Eventually, my blue face turned back to its normal color and breathing continued as it was meant to. No real harm done (except for the onset of claustrophobia). Still, I might have exercised the option of actually speaking to him about kissing at a later time. I chickened out.

Kissing doesn't always stop at the mouth, of course, nor do we want it too. The first lover I was with after Brett, the Second Lover in my life, would get so excited and turned on he would bite my nipples. A couple of times they actually bled (The Piranha). And

I? At twenty-two I was so young and inexperienced I didn't say anything. I thought that is what men do. I didn't know enough to protest. Shit, *if it hurts you, demand that he stop*!

Biting reminds me of my youth: Biting can be sexy. Over-biting can be cruel and will turn off your partner immediately (The Dracula Kisser). Instead, gently, tug at your partner's mouth ever so *slightly*. Nibble with your lips and teeth *playfully* on the earlobes or lips with no emphasis other than to let him fantasize about your mouth. *No more*. Relax and enjoy it when he does the same. I practiced that a lot in Paris. Sigh.

Granted, we all kiss a little differently. What is good for you might not be good for the next person. No one is perfect for everyone. You have to weed the garden before you find your favorite flower. A guy friend of mine, Michael, who was always promoting a sexual relationship (not to be confused with a real, *committed* relationship) talked with me about the women in his life and the men in mine. We talked about all sorts of things, actually. Kissing, naturally, came up.

"Men should know" I babbled on (brilliantly, I thought) about how important that first kiss is. If it is awful the woman will not want a repeat." Once we were at an outdoor evening concert and having a great time. Out of nowhere comes the kiss. Gads, *had he actually listened to me or did he always kiss that well*? His lips brushed mine tenderly and he didn't rush in where fools tread. It was gloriously compatible to mine. Our auras co-mingled as our lips co-mingled. It was total but sweet give and take (The Perfect Kisser). It made me, of course, covet more. We didn't hurry;

we just lived in that moment. It was sensual and teasing all at the same time. But I walked away from anything more. I was not interested in being one of his harem of women coming and going out of his bedroom door. Still, the memory of that perfect kiss lingers on...sigh again.

The chances are if you don't like your partner's kissing you will give up on considering anything further. Interesting, however, by my independent survey, some good kissers are not necessarily great in bed, and some bad kissers do better actually doing "The Deed". Still, if we are talking *quality* kissing, we need to hold the banner high. More quality! More time! Or, like Sally Field in the movie "Norma Rae", we stand up on the table and without a word hold up our sign: "Strike!"

OK, OK, I'll calm down.

Some of us, sadly, have been on strike far too long, anyway. Then what? Don't give up: Communication is everything, and having bared my soul to you about my past experiences walking away from bad FKs, I now pledge I will do my part to better express what I like (but not at the "kissing time"), *later and with diplomacy*. Heck, I guess I already started talking openly and honestly in Paris showing Jules just where to use that little gadget. So, once again, why not join my union: AF-KNO: The American Federation of Kissing and Nurturing Organization!

Another thing: No matter how old I am, I have always dreaded that First Kiss at the Door. All throughout the date you are wondering how that will go. *Don't wonder*. Don't worry and don't wait till saying goodnight at the door. If you are enjoying yourself, if your date is looking at you, leaning forward, move on it! Carpe diem! No tongues in mouth, though. I remember a Tom Cruise movie where he was kissing his girlfriend and the camera angle highlighted his tongue coming long out of his mouth (gads he has a long tongue...) and forging, slowly, into her mouth. It was all so prefabricated, so unreal, so staged. And it wasn't sexy, either. We get it. We get it. The tongue represents the penis, the girl's mouth the vagina. Hollywood didn't invent that thought. Contrastingly, remember when Keanu Reeves leaned over and lovingly kissed Diane Keaton in "Something's Gotta Give" on their first date? Hubba Hubba! OhmyGod, Keanu, you can lay your shoes under my bed any time! That man knew how to kiss. Maybe we can clone him.

The first kiss tells her that you are attracted and want to demonstrate that. That is not an old-fashioned concept. It is that spontaneous moment in Paris when I leaned across the table with Nick, meeting him half way and telling him I couldn't wait till later for the kiss. He loved it!

Many women want to feel we are good beings; we want men to feel we are, well, precious angels with no experience at all. Vestal virgins, each and every one of us. Make us feel that way while bringing out the devil in us and you are a genius. Women love for a man to frame his hands around her face, an acknowledgement of his devotion and her fragility. Yes, even if we are three hundred pounds, our hearts are fragile. Cupped hands on our face make us feel protected, safe, cherished. But be an angel yourself, gentlemen, and keep your kiss sweet by keeping your hands under control. It sets the tone for the evening.

If you seize the moment to kiss earlier in the date neither of you will worry about that anticipated First Kiss at the Front Door. I did that with Mel. As the evening dinner progressed at the restaurant, I knew throughout that I wanted him to kiss me. It was our third date; I had waited long enough. In the parking lot, safely tucked into the car, I sort of, well…blurted it out: "Let's just get that First Kiss over right now…so we don't have to wonder about it all the way home….that is, if you want to"(sophisticated aren't I?). Fortunately, he did. He smiled at me, vaguely amused that I was so up front about what we both were thinking, leaned over and kissed me. It was like valium; it immediately calmed my nerves down. When we got home I felt relaxed enough to invite him in for a cup of tea. Really, that was all I was offering at the moment, anyway. Mel didn't tell me he did not drink tea but he happily accepted the invitation sauntering through the front door.

Well, as you can guess, both of us wanted a repeat kiss, and then another, and another. We progressed from that First Kiss (in the car) into the Breathing Kiss within minutes. Hearing someone's aroused breathing is provocative in itself. We became lovers that night and for more than the next two years. He told me later that he loved hearing my breathing that first evening we became lovers. He could, he said, hear it change, becoming more aroused by his kisses as I breathed, deliberately, around his neck and earlobes. That turned him on all the more, which in turn, continued to turn me on. In between kissing we allowed for hugging, and Cheek Brushing (sort of our cheeks kissing each others cheeks). Again, we left time for anticipation by starting lightly and slowly building on that. Our spirits nurtured each other long before we headed for the bedroom.

Lips are a very sensual part in the body. There are many nerve endings in the lips. There are thirty-four facial muscles and a hundred and twelve postural muscles used during a kiss. Studies also indicate that prolonged kissing reduces stress and lowers your cholesterol. It should be part of your new health plan! The skin of the entire body, covered by more than four million sensory receptors, suggests you should spend a whole lot of productive time with each other kissing, well,... everywhere! Again, *it's just plain healthy*! Don't underestimate the importance of the mouth. Think of all the things your mouth (or his) does for you!

In Australia I visited a butterfly reserve. The caretaker explained to me that the male butterfly flutters around, non stop, when he courts the female for a full twenty-eight straight hours until she decides to accept him as a mate. How is that for persistence? (Of course, once mating is completed the male butterfly drops dead but let's not concentrate on that for now… he showed her a good time and that was his purpose in life, and an honorable one at that.) I used to give my kids butterfly kisses all the time, tracing their faces with my eyelashes and batting away. It was fun and ticklish. A girlfriend told me as a fully evolved woman, she was happy to encourage her partner to give her butterfly kisses in the small of her back, and he shouldn't hurry but live in the moment.

"OhmyGod", she happily reminiscenced! Flutter! Flutter! Yes, Yes, Yes!

European men oftentimes kiss a woman's hand first to see her reaction just like my Jules did. Obviously, if the woman immediately pulls away, one needn't proceed further. But if she doesn't, ooh la la! Jules would lightly trace my lips and mouth with his fingertip before kissing my lips. It tickles and those nerve endings stand up and take notice of what is to come. ("A kiss is the upper persuasion for a lower invasion."-unknown).

In France, they usually kiss the air around you from one side of the face to the other side. Normally, you needn't even feel the kiss. It is sort of setting an aura of positivity around that person. It is fun, affectionate and acknowledges you know this person. You could give it practically to anyone you know informally. Well, maybe not the maintenance man of your apartment building.

The French don't really claim French Kissing as their own invention, although they sure as hell practice it as much as Americans. But gads, some kissers are still better than others! Instead of trying to investigate my tonsils a man might try ever so gently to pry open my lips with his lips. If it is done carefully it is like having sex, just above the belly button, that's all. Way above. And if it is good you can give in to his kiss and welcome him in.

Men get bored with kissing. They want to move on. Practice a variety of kissing and he is less likely to get bored. Mix and Match. Variety *is* the spice of life.

Advanced Kissing 301 is the full body kiss, progressing on from one area to another. (*Warning! This rarely follows The First Kiss!*) Paul was an expert. He would trace my body with his lips and ever so lightly with his finger tips *slowly*, deliberately, watch my reaction. He knew enough to *not blow it by going down south for a very long time.* He would hold off for a long time touching or kissing everything *except* the "Magic Triangle" (figure it out). Instead, he would make me long for him to touch me there. The devil! He would tease me. He would love kissing my fingertips, hands, inside of my wrists, the inside of my elbows and back of my legs because he knew I loved it. Then he would kiss and suck on my toes, which is both creative and erotic. Damn, I had the cleanest feet in town.

Remember, that the skin is the largest organ of the body, covered with nerves to give you each more pleasure. But, if you have both pre-decided, as suggested earlier in this chapter, that is your abstinence day, just enjoy the journey, stay the course. Or not. What the hell, I won't kick you out of the Union if you change your mind and end up making mad, passionate love. I get it. I was young once. Hey, I still am!

When you take the time to kiss more you tell your partner that you value your time together. Nothing says that more than the time spent together, without TV, books, children, outside interferences. That time, that nurturing is ointment to the soul, the binding agent of your relationship. No members of the Kissing Hall of Shame, sil vous plait!

One last time: *No Propeller Kisses. No drooling or slobbering. No marks, no chapped mouth.* So, what do you say? Are you joining my union? Will you be a proud card-carrying member of the AF-KNO? After all you don't want to be the discouraging kiss of a young, upcoming actor like our Leo (or anyone else), do you?

Kissing is the one pure thing we can do in some format for the rest of our lives. That's the way I see it. I have come a long way, baby, from that first, innocent thirteen-year old kiss that sweet summer evening in Chicago half a century ago.

Twenty

Since my last visit to Paris, my philosophy on sex has changed. It is not because of the yo-yo men who wanted me as their "side-kick" but because of Jules.

Jules was honest with me from the get go. He recognized before I did what my needs would be in Paris. I would want to go out more than he could accommodate, either in time or financially. I would want to meet lots of people and I would be playing every day. He had to work a difficult job and was rarely available in the evenings. So, at his suggestion, I continued to meet other men. It was a good balance for me. He was my lover (although he didn't call it that) and they were courting me: every woman's dream: A Mormon in reverse!

But, if I am truly honest, not everything was smooth sailing with my young lover. It frustrated me to no end that we didn't spend many overnights together. It bothered me that I never saw where he lived or met any of his friends. Because of that I was always balancing the credibility of what he told me. Was I being gullible? Was he in a relationship elsewhere? Was it all just a big lie? I may have certainly dealt with our relationship in a different way had I all the pieces to the puzzle. But this was a fling, I reminded myself, nothing more. Do I really need to have a load of *requirements*?

One thing I should note is the practice of safe sex. I will give my young Parisian full credit for always sticking to safe sex. Once, as we started fooling around he apparently remembered he had not brought any condoms with him. All of a sudden he halted with our sweet endeavors. I could sense his spirit move away. Immediately, of course, I reacted. What was it? I asked him.

"Nothing" he answered with his thick French accent, shaking his head. So I continued on kissing him only to have him stop me.

"Maybe we can just relax and be with each other. Sometimes that is good, I think."

Hmmm.

"Don't be ridiculous. We don't have enough time together as it is." I started to kiss him again.

"Really, I am very content to just be with you. I am happy. Are you happy?"

I looked at him like he lost his mind.

"No, actually, I am not" I responded, perturbed with the situation. What was going on here?

"Let's go eat some lunch now" he suggested.

"I am not hungry" I pouted.

"Well, I am…" and he got up from the bed and headed towards the dinning room, where I had lunch prepared for us.

I slipped on a robe and joined him, fully perturbed, anxious and puzzled at what had just happened.

"I think we need to talk about this. What is going on? Are you turned off because of my stretch marks?" I babbled on, like the idiot I am. "I can't do anything about that; blame my children—" I blame everything on my stretch marks.

He reached for my hand and kissed it. "Do not make an issue where there is no issue". *Imagine me doing that?* "I just forgot my condoms, that is all. No big deal." The hell it wasn't! I sighed and reached for the salad.

After we had been seeing each other for a while I had a talk with him about why he was so careful. Did he have something I should know about?

"No, no", he replied, he was just protecting himself and me. *Himself?*

"Well", I retorted, "you are never going to have safer sex than you have with me that is for sure." He knew I was offended, wise young rascal that he was.

"Yes, but I did not know that before…."

"Well, you do now. So, do I need some protection from you?" He had told me by that time he was not seeing anyone else besides me. I was playing devil's advocate, I knew, since I was glad he was so careful.

"I just am used to using them. I cannot do it differently. It is what it is." I knew he was right, of course and I didn't want to take the conversation further. I realized it would get me into trouble if I didn't stop nagging. So, without lying to me he told me to let it go and enjoy what we had. I did but his credibility was beginning to disintegrate in front of my eyes.

I believe in giving people the benefit of the doubt. I don't always succeed at that but that is an issue I am working on. In philosopher Don Miguel Ruiz book "The Four Agreements" one of those agreements was not to make assumptions. That *always* gets me in trouble and everyone else I know. Without being naïve, why don't we give each other the benefit of the doubt more often? How much more peaceful our world would be. So in my quest for world peace I let the topic go.

It was what it was.

One night we were in bed and he started to talk to me about my feelings and leaving Paris. "Do you look forward to going back?" he queried me.

"No. No, I don't want to leave; I can't talk about it..." my voice sounded off, different.

"No. I can't talk about it, either." He said kissing me long and hard. I thought he was going to cry. "I can't tell you my feelings. You are going to leave me...."

His voice broke and we started to make love once again. That was the closest he ever came to telling me he loved me and I will remember that moment of the coming together of our hearts for a long time. It was very dear.

Jules was my advocate. I was in Paris long enough to need a haircut and color. I had a French woman hair stylist write down what the cost of that would be. But, when she finished my hair too dark, I needed then to have highlights done. How much could that cost? I didn't bother to ask nor did she bother to tell me. I assumed, since it didn't take her more than a couple of minutes of extra work that it wouldn't phase my original price. Wrong!

At the end of the cut, she *doubled* the cost because of the three-minute highlighting addition. It was outrageous. It was one of the few times I was so startled that I couldn't protest properly. He agreed and was bothered enough to ask me if I wanted him to go back and protest the charge. I knew I wouldn't see her again and off we trotted to the local hairdresser's.

Jules spoke to the owner and the hairdresser. He kept his cool and tried negotiating for me but he couldn't get them to budge. So, he took photos of the outside of the shop with his phone and told them he would plaster it on the internet. The owner was angry, of course, but so were we.

Another time, in an effort to keep up with the boot fashion in Paris I purchased a pair of boots. Boots, shoes and everything else are double and triple what we would pay for in America for similar quality. Still,

I felt compelled to buy some boots. Everyone in Paris wore boots. And they would keep me warm as the winter approached. Unfortunately, they soon pinched my feet in spite of the high price tag. I told Jules. Off he drove us to the shop to confront the French sales people. Always a gentleman, trying his best, he finally had to give up on the French women who were out to make their own statement: No exchanges! No returns!

For me and for Jules it was frustrating. He didn't want his city's reputation diminished in my eyes. And I didn't want to appear to be a brisk, rude American so he became my intermediary, my advocate. Bless his little, Gaulish heart.

"It's not so much that they are saying no" I remarked, "but the nasty way they say it."

Jules nodded, embarrassed. He wanted me to see the best of Paris but the silly bureaucracy was irritating. Still, he was always looking after me and that attention and effort I truly loved.

He was a bit of an old-fashioned gentleman even at his young age but layer-by-layer, week after week, however, I noticed slight changes in his behavior. As the younger of the couple, he felt uncomfortable with anything that smacked of "motherly" wisdom. He would jump and say something like "I'm sorry I am not fifty! Perhaps, I wouldn't do that, then. I would make you more happy!" It was adolescent but I recognized he was trying to hold his own with an older, more sophisticated woman than he was man. Most of the time he pulled it off but not always.

It irked me to no end that he waited to the last minute to call me for a date or get-together. He admitted he was not good at dating etiquette. *No kidding*. But it meant I had to reshuffle my schedule to accommodate him or I would be gone and he would not be able to reach me that day. It bugged me to no end.

I wanted more sex and more time….in that order. My guess was he did, as well. After all, the guy was practically just out of kindergarten. OK, OK. He wasn't that young, but do you remember what you were like – hormonally, at thirty?

So adjustments were constantly being made on both our parts. It was hard to decide if his attitude was changing or not. Because he was so reserved and often held back affection publicly I didn't notice when he actually did start to pull away. One day in his car (we were in his car too much if you asked me) I leaned over and started kissing him on the neck.

"Don't kiss me!" he retorted like I was a pesty fly on his cheek, clearly irritated with me. "I am trying to drive!" *Don't kiss me?* What the hell was going on here? I laughed. I thought he was kidding. "It is not funny. I might get in an accident" he huffed (a French huff, at that).

Something was going on. He hadn't seemed happy in a couple of days but I couldn't drag it out of him. Men just regress into their caves. If they don't want to talk about something there is no woman on the face of the earth who can make them talk. Hmmm.

Eventually, fairly late, he got me home mid afternoon. We had not yet had lunch and I invited him to have some of my fabulous (if I do say so) homemade quiche. I love to cook and entertain. Food is such a common denominator. I have always nurtured this way. It is the way I express my love and caring for those in my life. I attended professional culinary schools in the U.S. and Europe. I know what I am doing.

He hemmed and hawed and then took a phone call as he parked his car motioning me to get out and that he would meet me at my apartment. What was he hiding, I thought? Why couldn't I listen to the conversation? I would only be able to interpret one out of ten words, anyway.

Perturbed, I got out. Something was going on. He hadn't offered to take me to lunch. He had to get to his job within an hour and he was dismissive. Red flags, red flags everywhere.

When he came up to my apartment he said he would eat his quiche cold because he didn't have any time to wait for the oven to heat up. So, he sat at the dining room table and ate while I just sat there without any food. He said nothing. I tried, as I always did, to elicit some word of appreciation, of delight in enjoying my cuisine. This lack of manners bothered the hell out of me. I was still steaming about the "Don't kiss me!" remark. I put my heart into my food. Is it so much to ask someone to tell me it is delicious and thank you? Oui! Apparently so.

When I tried to engage him in conversation and he would not respond I was further incensed. "The least you could do is tell me you like it!" The argument built. "I took some time to do it, after all."

"It took you thirty minutes to make" he shrugged, still not expressing any appreciation. With that I got up, looked at him and told him how I felt: "You are being a real jerk!" and I huffed off to the kitchen to get my warmed quiche. He sat there and did not answer. Silence. Silence is not really silence, is it? It speaks volumes.

I was pissed. I cleaned up the kitchen and then cleared the dinning room table with not a word passing between us.

Finally, I said "I think it is time for you to go."

He agreed, jumped up and I walked him to the door. He walked out and looked at me. I didn't say another word. I shook my head and closed the door.

Jules was gone.

Men don't give exit interviews, do they? There is no opportunity for "closure". Women would like to know why and that question is rarely addressed. There could be any number of reasons, imagined and real: he could have been in love with me and watched as the departure date approached making him push away from me. He could have been involved with someone else. The age and cultural differences might have been too huge for him to handle. He knew I was pressuring him to see his apartment and he had not yet come across with that. Who the heck knows? It all happened so quickly. Speed is the getaway plan. It stinks, basically. Whatever the reason, good, bad or indifferent, I still would have preferred to understand his thinking.

I sent him two emails before I left ten days later inviting him to come and talk to me. He never answered them. I left my beloved Paris without having seen or heard from him again.

Going from being lovers to nothing in the blink of an eye is a big loss. I am old-fashioned enough to know that sharing my thoughts, my dreams, hell, my fabulous bod with someone is a privilege to be experienced with someone who understands it is a privilege. Then, pouff, it is over. It is no more. Did it ever exist? Did I dream this? The emotional extremes can be formidable.

I hate for any relationship to end on a sour note. It just felt sort of lousy to have him treat me so disrespectfully in the end. But when I think of Jules I still smile. I will always recall his thoughtfulness, his kindnesses, and his sexual enthusiasm in bed. I was drawn to the very intimacy of my relationship with Jules and enjoyed his company enormously. The sex renewed my zest, that enjoyment that I hadn't had for years. Nitric Oxide, indeed! It freed me. It allowed me to enjoy others on different levels with no one to hold me back. It refreshed and awakened me. The arrangement had been, I hope, mutually satisfying to us both. Most of my needs were met and so were his.

Most of all, I will recall that for the majority of my time in Paris he was a dear friend. If I could say that about all my former lovers, I would be a most blessed woman. Heck, I am blessed. Despite that.

Twenty-One

The City of Lights was changing. The cool autumn air ushered in the winter winds. Leafs had long since fallen off the trees and what was once an oasis of color stood long, lean, barren limbs where lush arbor trails once lead me. I love the fall in Paris. All that endless walking transformed my figure and I was five pounds thinner (even with all the eating) than when I arrived.

But, unexpectedly, I found there was a mystique to Winter Paris. The cafes, which line endless avenues and streets now hung heavy plastic sheets on the outside and coupled that up with heaters to keep patrons warm and cozy. Little, charming cafes, endless boutique stops now welcomed visitors with frost nipping at the window pains. Lit candles added an extra glow of warmth, a beaconing to come in and warm yourself. Now I learned to love walking in Winter Paris. It seemed, in a way, even more romantic than autumn.

As I approached Thanksgiving I considered how I should celebrate. I considered the hoggishness of Thanksgiving and decided to share with those who did not enjoy the same abundance as I. Over the decades that I have visited Paris I have never before noticed so many beggars. They were everywhere. Most of them were not French; they were immigrants from Eastern countries who, in speaking no other language but their own, seemed doomed to poverty.

But because there were so many I had decided to just ignore them. I was always at odds with this decision even back in California. Was I really helping someone or encouraging him to beg? It is a question I still cannot answer. But I was not going to ignore them now, not on Thanksgiving. It was time to melt my heart.

On Thanksgiving I set out early morning with my mobile grocery cart that all French use to wheel to their marketplaces. It was filled with fruit and my pockets filled with euros. Apparently, wherever the homeless sleep it generally is not directly on the streets unless they have passed out from alcohol consumption. I could not find any homeless anywhere. I returned home befuddled, tired with an undistributed fruit-filled cart. I was fasting for the day. I had wanted to see what hunger felt like if I lived in Paris. So I had a cup of tea to warm myself, rested and then once again headed back out to find all those poor, suffering souls who have to swallow their pride and beg for money.

Of course, by noon they were everywhere most especially in the tourists districts. Over and over I handed a euro or two along with a piece of fruit without hesitation. Wisps of delicious French food wafted through the air. My stomach growled and I recognized, as I had not before, that the difficulty of being hungry in Paris must be compounded with the fact that there are so many restaurants, creperies, bars, bistros, compounding, torturing really, the senses of the hungry and homeless.

I returned to my apartment about 6 PM, cold, tired from hours of walking but satisfied. I fixed myself a plate of lentils and rice and a cup of tea and thanked the Almighty that I did not have to worry about food on my plate. It was a delicious Thanksgiving, well spent, and one I would repeat any year I was in Paris.

As Thanksgiving approached the holidays ahead became obvious. Near the north end of Tulleries Garden by Place de la Concorde, a mammoth "Ferris Wheel", La Grande Roue, was erected. A Frenchman told me, "It is really for the tourists, not us". It stood almost 200' tall. It had warm, enclosed cabins and I sauntered over one evening to have a closer look. I kurplunked a whopping twelve euro and jumped on board with a couple from Germany. Slowly, very slowly, our cabin made its way up providing panoramic views of nighttime Winter Paris, of twinkling lights from Champs-Elysees and the barren grounds of Winter Tullieries Gardens. In fairness we were in our cabin almost fifteen minutes but doing it alone was not exactly as fun as cuddling with a honey, was it?

Off I trotted to take a photo of some silly, holiday prop at the exit of the ride where venders were offering paid-for photos. The man saw me, jumped in front of his precious, silly plastic prop and waved at me to go away. I could not take a photo. Apparently, his prop was most sacred not because of the symbolism of the holiday but because it represented his profits. Baa Humbug!!

Along the east end on both sides of the Champs-Elysees every year they erect a holiday village, little sheds adorned with holiday decorations, each brimming over with gifts, candies, snacks, and other goodies. These shops lined both sides of the avenue.

It attracted not only the tourists but the French, as well, as families trotted their tots and dogs (in France especially they were considered family members, too, after all) around to view a moose, which masqueraded as a reindeer, ride a kiddy cart, and buy sweets. Well, I couldn't fit myself into a kiddy cart but I sure enjoyed tasting such delectable as chocolate covered raspberries kabob. Where they got raspberries from, so out of season, I will never know. I queued up like everyone else for other goodies. I had a salmon over the grill on a bun and it tasted so good I went back for more. Finishing up with hot chocolate, I then bought some caviar to take home. I was, indeed, getting into the holiday spirit.

One thing I noticed as I ventured around Paris was the lack of nativity scenes anywhere. Not at Notre Dame or any of the well-known churches, not in the shop windows. Nowhere. It bugged me. French use any excuse, religious or otherwise, to take an extra day or two of "religious" holiday but they didn't seem to recognize and honor what the holiday was all about. Even though many well known cathedrals and churches were owned by the government, would it have been so difficult for the government to acknowledge what these historic buildings represented? Apparently so.

I visited several areas of Paris by foot, really the best way to see any city. In one area near St Madeleine Church, shops were decorated with red-flocked

Christmas trees and black ornaments. They were about the gaudiest things I could imagine.

I hurried my way over to Galleries Lafayette to see their window and light displays. While it wasn't as elaborate as we have in the United States, the windows were full of cute little scenes of moving teddy bears; the blinking lights wrapped around the store on rue Haussmann. Inside, there was a humongous Christmas tree that stood in the center of the store under a thirty-three meter high-glassed doom. There were ten painted, decorated windows encapsulated in metal frames inside the store. This signature store opened at the end of the Belle Epilogue era in 1913. Especially complimenting it was the gorgeous gold relief adorning each level of the store, walls, balconies, banisters and overviews. Over-sized gift boxes, suspended from the ceiling by invisible wire, gave the feeling of magical, floating surprises waiting to be opened. It was rich and warm and welcoming.

But it wasn't home. I was beginning to get antsy. It soon would be time to return to the states and I walked each neighborhood bidding it adieu. I said good-bye to the rues I loved so well, good-bye to the boutiques and chocolatiers, and even bid good-bye to my favorite farmers at my local Open Air Market, which I visited twice a week for months.

Twenty-Two

My new American girlfriend, Robin, who was living in Paris for three years, decided to join me on my last weekend in Paris at a splurge restaurant that we each had always wanted to try: La Tour d' Argent. It was the end of my long, expensive Parisian adventure and I wanted to finish it all off and have something to look forward to till the moment of my departure. Once I heard they served brunch, I reserved a table for us.

The Saturday morning before I departed, I took a long walk around Notre Dame, another favorite building in Paris, meandered across the bridge and off to the restaurant to meet Robin. A doorman, the manager and the hat check lady were there to meet and greet me, take my coat and escort me through the lovely living room and bar area on the first floor up the elevator where the restaurant was. It was a well-orchestrated ritual with someone calling the upstairs matri'd to tell him the name of the next patron arriving so he could greet me by name.

The view from the large glass windows of the Seine was magnificent. It must be that much better at nighttime, I thought. The restaurant itself was a model of classic French etiquette. A variety of stewards, waiters, and busboys stood at attention like little nutcrackers at their stations ready to jump at the snap of a finger. If I am honest, however, I thought the restaurant needed a bit of a restoration as it appeared just a bit old and slightly shabby.

Robin arrived and we ordered champagne while we looked at the prix set menu (65 euros). Tiny appetizers started to arrive gratis of the chef. Then one course after another tantalized our palette. The restaurant décor started to look better, cleaner and opulent. We relaxed, unhurried, enjoying every morsel we devoured. I ordered cepes stuffed with foie gras. By the time I finished it I told my waiter that I loved him. I was in ecstasy, you see. I couldn't help myself. He seemed to sparkle after that knowing that he was pleasing me. Everyone needs to hear they are loved; my waiter no exception.

My N.O. levels were off the charts. I ordered their specialty duck. This restaurant actually owns and operates its own duck farm. As I savored every luscious piece of duck and slurped down another glass of champagne, I discovered that I didn't want to swallow. I wanted to savor those creative, fabulous flavors in my mouth forever. My waiter, looking somewhat like Alfred Hitchcock, proudly delivered a card on a silver platter. Yep, they gave me the duck's life certification on a souvenir card! I was actually receiving a certification of my duck's life (!) that he gave to a noble cause: mon pleasure!

"But my duck must have a name!" I teased.

"We ran out of names" Henry, stated, acting disappointed for me.

"Then I shall name him after you, Henry. My duck's name is Henry!" I declared, quite in the moment.

"Very well, madam!" he found me amusing. See I can amuse a Frenchman or two, even at my age.

When Henry, the waiter cleared our table, he had joked that I had eaten old Henry very well. "You have eaten me!" he chuckled quietly, now well into our American humor.

"In a manner of speaking" I giggled, a bit surprised as his risqué reference but knowing he felt relaxed enough with a probable fifty-year tenure at his station and our crazy American ways to enjoy a humorous moment with his guest. Who says the French don't have a sense of humor?

Next they surprised us with French cookies and a variety of specialties to enjoy prior to our ordered desserts. Then, they presented chocolates. Well, this is my idea of heaven, I have to tell you. If we shape our own heaven when we die this is where I want to go. With a tab to each of us of about $150, you might say heaven is a really good but still a splurge buy!

I took a train and was home in five minutes. My final event in Paris was that last Saturday night. It was a violin concert at Eglise de St. Madeline complete with a beautiful young opera singer dressed to the hilt. St Madeleine Church was a huge, Napoleonic structure built in the late 1700s. It was filled to capacity and Mozart's Requiem never sounded so perfect. As I sat in this, my final concert, my heart overflowed with an appreciation for the abundance in my life.

I was packed and ready to go and I knew it wouldn't be long before I was back.

Sometimes re-entry to home and hearth is a bit staid, almost a let down from the glamour of such a rejuvenating trip. But with my adrenaline levels (Nitric Oxide, God bless it!) brimming over, I got off the plane in LA with no regrets. Not one. Not Jules. Not any of the goofy guys I met. Not any of the operas, ballets, or concerts I attended. Not one meal. I had recovered. I looked at my son and daughter and hugged them, hungry to hear about their lives because mine was so very much in order.

But I have to tell you a secret: I was already planning my return.

PART II

Twenty-Three

I arrived back in Paris at the beginning of May, stepped off the plane, inhaled my first breath of forty-degree air and wondered when, exactly, spring arrived. It was the "lusty month of May" for Pete's sake! I hadn't envisioned the need for heavy winter clothes. I was back for another three months of boosting my Nitric Oxide levels. When I arrived home the previous December I was filled with the spirit of my Parisian adventures. It lasted through the holidays and then some. It was that natural high we all want but often don't experience without the aid of things we shouldn't consume. I still retain some of it. Residual N.O., I call it. Paris, nitric oxide and middle-aged renewal were, for me, all related. You get some and you want more. I guess I am a glutton for pleasure! *A Pleasure Glutton*; I think I just coined a new word! The proud card-carrying founder of the AF-KNO (American Federation of Kissing and Nurturing Organization).

I wanted more, more, more of everything! Was that so much to expect? I suppose you are not really surprised at that, are you? But could I repeat the same scenario by sheer will power? I didn't know it at the time but my experiences would be quite different than the autumn trip.

So, where was I? Oh, yes, May 5 and forty degrees. Burr! Baby, it's cold outside! I was totally unprepared for winter weather with open-toed shoes and summer clothes. I had been delighted as I packed that I didn't have to consider the weight and thickness of winter coats, boots, sweaters etc. as on my last trip. Or so I thought. Bienvenue to "spring" in Paris! "Tra la, tra la, the lusty month of May"? More like "Button up your overcoat". Unfortunately, this California girl did not have an overcoat! But be careful of what you wish for, the weather would change quite often even within a one day context for quite a long time. If we are singing here, remember the song "I love Paris in the springtime, I love Paris in the fall, I love Paris in the summer, I love Paris..."? Yada yada. Who would have known they could all fall on the same day!

I didn't return to the apartment by the Eiffel Tower. I am allergic to wool and feathers; I had warned the landlady, before signing my lease with a rental agency in New York, of that fact. But the she ignored that and lied to them and to me. Her living room furniture was not just old and uncomfortable but was stuffed with feathers. Ahchoo! I had paid in full the entire three-month's rent so I was unable to move from an apartment that didn't allow me to sit in the living room! She simply wouldn't return my money. French Witch. Still, it was a cute apartment in a neighborhood I liked and it was near, as you know by now, to my beloved Eiffel Tower, filled as it always was with good luck and sparkling lights.

In November I found an apartment in the nineteenth arrondissement for my upcoming spring stay. It was a stunning two-bedroom apartment with a huge, oversized dinning room, two bathrooms, a modern kitchen and two patios, a beautiful one in the front and one off the kitchen. I loved the apartment. It was by a canal and a park and I thought I was quite clever in negotiating the rent. That should have been a clue; very few landlords in Paris ever negotiate. Had I known that (and more) at the time I would have given second thought to the whole "deal".

What I hadn't seriously considered in my inspection of the apartment and area was how horribly hot the summertime weather would be and the potential consequences to living far out of central Paris. Nor did I correctly understand how much hotter and more crowded the metro would be. It would be a serious miscalculation on my part. Planning to go to hell? Hell is located in the summer Paris metro.

I suppose, as I was reminded by my son, that it is often impossible to go back to the scene of a fabulous vacation and relive it again as it had been. He was partially right.

On many levels the new vacation would be challenged by impossible weather and a variety of other maladies. My psyche is steered by weather and food. You already knew about the culinary aspect. In California, we are all, basically, weather wusses, migrating from other states' extreme weather conditions. I am no exception. I know extreme weather when I see it. I had lived in Chicago and I know now I am not a polar bear. I had lived in the desert (I am convinced they are all reptiles from another planet). So location, location, location; it is no wonder I chose to live in southern California. But choosing to live so far out of central Paris would end up problematic.

There were pluses to my neighborhood, the nineteenth, however. It had the picturesque canal St Martin running up from the Bastille, lined with bike and walking paths, which passed my area and stretched out into the forests. I knew I would take advantage of that availability. There was a huge park, parc de la Villette, two blocks away paralleling the canal. I could hear free concerts from my patio every weekend; they attracted a multitude of locals. It was filled with loads of children's areas, a carousel, a café, a few large museums, a conservatorie of music and huge, modernistic "sculptures" throughout the park. For a visitor it could be a lovely weekend destination on the bike path ending in a day at the park.

Not too far away, certainly walking distance for me, was my favorite park in Paris, parc des Buttes Chaumont. Before Haussmann rebuilt it, it was a garbage dump. Seriously. But, no more. It was a gorgeous, hilly, well-landscaped park with ponds and walk bridges, breathtaking in beauty and a lovely walking destination for everyone.

Fun, unexpected things would occur in my new neighborhood. One day when the rain finally ended, I walked towards the metro to find a huge gathered crowd of spectators enjoying a parade marching down the street, three blocks from my apartment. I was told it was "Carnival". Never mind that it was May; it was Carnival time!

Another time, the neighborhood set up a charming, little outer city block party/flea market, complete with its own little parade, music and clowns. I totally stumbled on that and enjoyed every moment.

My neighborhood in the fifteenth, near the Eiffel Tower, did also have charming little surprises. Every Wednesday afternoon a mariachi band would come wending its way down my street and people would come out on their terraces to hear them. We threw euros down at them, which they happily caught in their sombreros and in ten minutes they were gone. I loved to be home on Wednesday afternoons! Ole!

Now, in the nineteenth, it was a whole different atmosphere. But there was still some music. On my block there lived an opera singer who practiced her scales every morning and evening. Sometimes, men would yell something nasty in French out the window at her. Idiots. I wish I could have met her; she really added to the dimension of my experience. There was a piano teacher whose music filled the air. There were good things in the nineteenth, undoubtedly.

My new neighborhood was filled with a kaleidoscope of cultures, races and religious diversity. There were countless Hasidic Jews with their high black hats, long beards and curly payots hanging from the side of their faces. There were Muslims of all nationalities and Africans dressed in colorful tribal attire. Because there were so many holy days (translate: holidays) there must have been a major influx of Christians somewhere, although there didn't appear to be many churches. It promised to be a true, international experience. For me, that had allure.

But not all international experiences were comfortable. I became unsettled with many of my Muslim neighbors. Even in the extreme heat, the women were wrapped in layers of heavy clothing while their men, wearing short sleeve shirts and breezy fabrics walked beside them. I rarely saw Muslim women smile. I never saw them talking to their husbands. I sometimes saw men with very short whips, slingshot-size, discreetly slapping their women as they berated them publicly. The women lowered their heads and never spoke a word. It was all my undisciplined Irish self could do to keep from injecting my two cents worth (probably starting an international incident).

I didn't want to be a target, either, or to further jeopardize the "well-being" of my Muslim sisters. The only time I ever saw them smile, and that was only occasionally, was when they were watching their children play. Even, then, they were mothering an average of five children, much more than the rest of the world took on and the poor dears had to be exhausted, hot and unhappy. I am sure there were modern Muslims but they usually didn't emanate from the Eastern countries, where women appeared to be allowed such limited scope.

After a constant, habitual change of weather from freezing cold, to rainy, to hot, to cold again, to rainy I became disenchanted. Imagine me discontented in Paris! It was a phenomenon. I didn't know what to do with those raw feelings. I would embark on those metros, stuffed with people, many who didn't understand the meaning of good hygiene, profusely sweating myself like a cochon (pig) and wondered if I could make it to my connection without vomiting. Am I having fun yet, I wondered?

The metros out of central Paris were an entirely different experience than I had the previous fall. For one thing, my beloved musicians and talented singers did not frequent them often. Oh, and did I miss their strains of music lifting my mood wherever I was. I must have been a musician in another life. The creative arts in Paris are fantastic. They continually breathed life into my spirit. My serotonins danced along with the music.

In the fifteenth arrondissement I got to know the musicians on my metro line. I recognized them and their musical selections. Transfer to another line and there were a different set of vocalists, musicians and puppeteers. When a new entertainer was added to the mix everyone knew. They auditioned and were licensed by the government so the caliber of talent could often be quite high. Some were just creative. One puppeteer set up in three seconds his "stage" on my metro car. He spread a sheet that connected from one pole on the train car to the other, clicked on a recording "Speedy Gonzales" and hid behind the sheet while his little Mexican puppet (complete with sombrero) danced around the sheet. He captured the hearts of everyone that day. I wonder if he knew it. I wonder if any of them fully understand how much delight they add to every day living in Paris? If they made me smile (not difficult) they got a tip. It doubled my metro fares but it also doubled my pleasure.

Instead, now in the nineteenth, daily beggars would come on to the metros from my area and announce

"Bonjour, Madams, Messieurs..." and go into their schlep about their hard lives, turn of events and other reasons to solicit sympathy and, in turn, money. Some of them were teenagers. They would stand in the crowded metro, noises filling the air and talk right through it all, without raising their voices, for sometimes three full minutes. Sometimes, someone would jar my interest. For instance, a neatly dressed Chinese man stood in front of the metro passengers and repeated his plea (in French, of course) for help. It is unusual for Chinese to beg. They have a lot of pride. I felt sorry for him but not sorry enough to hand over my lunch money. Daily, I listened to the beggars instead of my beloved musicians and I grew resentful of their intrusion into my space. I became unsettled with the area in which I lived and I had no one to blame but myself.

Of course, most underground metros are not air-conditioned. Every time I exited the metro I felt like I had just emerged from the shower, sweat pouring down my face, boobs and back. Even my panties were wet and this time it was not sexy. I liked to think that those sweltering metro trips were my personal detox program. I reasoned that I would sweat out all the calories I consumed *without exercise*. That was my new health plan. Hot weather makes me lethargic. My exercise routine quickly evaporated as I struggled to survive hot, humid days both above the ground and below.

Air conditioning anywhere is an upscale privilege, particularly in homes. The French always came up with the same reason not to have air-conditioned apartment buildings: pollution. But the pollution of the traffic never seemed to be a concern. Be that as it may, one could find an interesting "air conditioner" at stores, quite pricey by our standards; it would help to cool a room but not the entire apartment. It was a large box supporting a sort of long, ungainly, over-sized washer/dryer-type hose that literally stuck out the window. The window would be shut as much as possible with perhaps towels on the bottom to try to prevent hot air from coming in. Of course, this didn't work well but it was considered a luxury. My apartment building was barely ten years old and none of it was centrally air-conditioned.

The first week I was there my elevator broke down for the weekend. I had to scale seven floors in high humidity with ninety plus weather. One time I did it four times in one day, a full twenty-eight story building! I suppose it gave me my exercise that day but if you were older, carting children or carrying bags it was particularly formidable. But this is Paris; old and new problems are often the same. One was suppose to "embrace" it, I was told by my French friends. Hmmm.

Of course, there were problems in central Paris' transit system, as well. Tourists really must not be naïve about pickpockets in the *central* corridor of the Paris Metro system. Cling to your purses, bags, cameras and pockets! Why? I witnessed pickpockets at work several times. They often travel in gangs. Young girls, for instance, from Eastern countries would try to distract a person on the metro while another one of the gang would grab something as the metro doors open. Well, they would have to kill me before they got one euro, I vowed. I worked way too hard to loose my moula to a band of thieves from across the border. They did once surround me, pushing into me but I was on to them. Slinging my purse straps over my shoulder, across my chest and holding on for dear life, I discouraged them and I watched them move on to someone else.

Beyond the heat, crowds and partial but frequent rail strikes, there was ample reason to *stay central*. It was simply more convenient. If there is nothing else you learn from my memoir, learn this: *Stay Central Paris*. Sacrifice the space, save a little more moula for a Central Paris apartment. You will be happier. I guarantee it.

Nonetheless, in spite of my new neighborhood, I was determined to have another unique vacation and that would begin my first evening in Paris. A week before I had left Paris the previous November, I was offered a free membership in ParisCatch.com, who was merging with a website in Paris called Meetig. My French friends came over to my apartment and guided me through the French instructions for putting up my profile. They had met and married via a similar website so they were very excited at my starting a new membership. That done, I sat back in California for six months and let the French fellows find me via that website. I had more than a dozen lined up to meet before I stepped off the plane. I was prepared, or so I thought, for a hell of a good time.

OK, I have kept you waiting long enough. How were the men going to compare to my autumn experiences? Eight hours after my arrival, I had a rendezvous with my first man from Meetig, who had invited me for drinks and dinner. That worked for me! Food speaks an international language, doesn't it?

Twenty-Four

His name was Mehmet. He was originally from Turkey and had been in Paris for decades. He was waiting for me on the outside patio of Le Café de Flore, a place where Picasso was a regular (Picasso and Hemingway really got around) and directly next door to the even more famous, Les Deux Magots. I took the metro down to the sixth arrondissement and hurried to meet him, knowing full well I didn't look my best (to put it mildly). I had borrowed a dirty suede coat from my new landlady and, frankly, was grateful even for that. She was a size smaller but I snuggled into that winter jacket with nothing but gratitude. My open-toed summer shoes made me look a little like an immigrant from the New World, which was exactly what I was. Humbling. Still, it was survival of the fittest: I needed warmth and was wholly unprepared for the cold "spring" night air. What's a girl to do?

Mehmet was a well-dressed businessman who lived in Versailles. He spoke excellent English. We huddled under the restaurant canopy and had a glass of wine. I felt delighted to be out on my first night in Paris. Would it be a good omen?

After wine, he escorted me over to a small restaurant in the sixth and we dined and chatted for the next few hours. There are endless little cafes and bistros throughout Paris but hurrying through the side rues of Paris was always a very quaint experience. As the damp, dark weather enfolded us we reached our destination and hurried in. He ordered a bottle of Domaine Des Billards Saint-Amour (Saint of Love) to honor my arrival in Paris. No kidding. I loved it, of course. I am sure it had nothing to do with the name. Really. *Pour me another one, Cher.* I assume it was named after a very favorite saint in France. Either way, leave it to the French to name a wine that has to be a knock out big seller just because of the label. Mehmet really was a nice man, very conversant, intelligent and I looked forward to see him again. The conversation flowed and he already began to encourage me to get out of the nineteenth; he didn't think it safe. He would help me, he promised.

But it was the first in a string of bazaar dating experiences, directly opposite to the Paris I experienced the previous fall. Inadvertently, I must have angered the Paris Gods. Even though Mehmet was charming and attentive I never saw him again. I blame it, of course, on that dirty suede coat. Why should guy like that want to date an "immigrant"?

One of my earliest dates, a Frenchman I met through Meetig, asked if I would like to go to a wine tasting at the le Bourse, Paris' stock exchange. It normally is not opened to the public so it would be a wonderful opportunity to view the inside of the building, he declared. He had me at wine tasting.

We met as he parked his motorcycle across the street from the Bourse and we entered together. It was the shortest date of my life. We started off with his favorite reds but when it became apparent I preferred champagne he encouraged me to go off on my own. I did and he became the second in a long line of disappearing Frenchmen. The Paris Gods would blast several men off the face of the earth in that first month. I would never see or hear from those men again. Was the Great Houdini alive? I felt I should forewarn their family members of their imminent disappearance as I planned each new date only to be stood up at some miscommunication along the path. Did I have spinach in my teeth? Still, on that day I managed to meander my way through three rooms of French wines and drinkers. I had a great time on my own. Sante! (Cheers!)

I have never had a good memory for names. Never. When I was about thirty years old my husband and I were having a dinner party and I had a brain freeze; I couldn't remember the name of one person in the room. What did I do? Well, there is great comedy in truth sometimes. I simply announced to everyone in the room that I couldn't remember their names and would they please introduce themselves to each other. I was thirty then. It was funny. But at sixty-something it was a little too close to the old fogies' home. One day they will find me stumbling my way down Rue Mouffard in my nightie speaking an odd, pigeon mix of French and English and asking where I am and who I am. It is only a matter of time.

I have to admit I was becoming wary of French names. It was damn confusing when I started to meet men with the same names. There were two Jean Louis, two Louis Phillips, three Phillips, one Jean, and two Georges Phillips. What abundance! OK, over abundance. Each would call me and not identify who they were or did so in such a fast manner that I couldn't get the name (or didn't know which Jean

Louis it was!). Then, embarrassed, I would punt through the conversation hoping to figure it all out.

Once, one of the men stated with exasperation:

"But you have given me your phone number! How do you *not* know who this is?"

Just as exasperated I would put the truth right out there: "Do you think you are the only Frenchmen I have shared my phone number with?"

It didn't make for a good beginning.

And I? I must have appeared totally nuts to the French gents. Nothing new, I guessed. I was American. Weren't all Americans a little crazy? I felt a little dizzy with it all. What the heck was the matter with me? Had dementia arrived?

It wasn't till some time later that I considered my situation. I felt dizzy because *there was no balance in my life again!* Was balance important on the dating scene? You betcha. It was all just *too much*. Too many boxes of chocolate make you sick. Prior to my last trip I felt that balance was necessary because of the difficult challenges of every day living (whatever they might be for each of us). I had never considered that dating too much was as formidable as too many crises. It was all about balance. It was a cathartic moment.

Eventually, I decided to not allow many of them to pursue me, to just get back to what I originally came to Paris for: the arts. That decision didn't prohibit me from meeting others. However, I continued with much less emphasis meeting new men. But dating websites have never really been my forte. They were compounded with language issues (in Paris, anyway) and seemed to attract insincere players. Dating had lots its charm and I wanted my balance back.

Twenty-Five

There are an endless myriad of events happening in Paris year round, wonderful, outdoor festivals such as the Fete de la Musique in June or the Le Journee Du Patrimonie throughout Europe in late September or la Plages in July/August.

One June evening every year throughout the city there are scheduled concerts and spontaneous musicians and bands, which ease one's troubled soul, if one did, indeed, have a troubled soul. Certainly, the music enlivens the heartbeat of Paris till the wee hours of the morning. The residents, tourists and students cram the streets, drinking and dancing and having an awesome time.

I had planned a dinner date in the fifth arrondissement near the Pantheon with an American I had met on line. Tiny, narrow streets and enticing cafes persuade you to become part of a picture postcard scene. In front of Restaurant La Maison de Verlaine, on rue Mouffertard, hung a plaque commemorating that the Poet, Paul Verlaine, lived and eventually died there in 1844 (hopefully not at my table). More recently (and for the Americans) another plaque stated that Hemingway lived there from 1921-1924 (as I have said the man got around). I normally never went to these types of restaurants because most are tourist traps, webs if you will, luring in the tourists with fanciful curbside appeal and then providing poor service and disappointing fare.

Restaurant La Maison de Verlaine was another one of those adorable French restaurants with red checkered table cloths, candles and flowers on the tiny tables. I couldn't and didn't want to resist it; that seemed to be my growing sentiment about most things French... (*but not all*). It had both an indoor café and an outdoor patio where we could sip our wine and enjoy our meal while we watched the perpetual crowds prowling the streets looking for free music on corner after corner, square after square. Surprisingly, the food was better than expected, service acceptable and menu moderately priced. It was perfect for this visiting American and me and we enjoyed ourselves immensely. It was a beautiful summer evening sans the rain and humidity and we sat there for some time enjoying the scene, living in the moment.

Then we joined the students for a brief interchange, had our photos taken and danced enough to let them know we weren't ready for the grave any time soon.

The previous September I stumbled upon Le Journee Du Patriomonie, a celebration throughout Europe when, for two days, most government buildings and museums were opened gratis to the public. My first choice was the Assemble Nationale, the lower house of the French Parliament, not far from the Eiffel Tower. It was the only place on the list for that weekend (other than the presidential palace) that normally is never opened to the public. So, off I went early in the morning to queue up with all French. I was, at least at that time, the only English-speaking visitor in line.

I will always remember this visit, this place and this day. It was my first choice and it turned out to be my favorite one. Assemble Nationale was absolutely exquisite in décor and its' personnel welcomed with open arms each and every visitor. I found the Republican Guards (honorary security guards) ready, willing and able to take my photo. Almost everyone spoke some English and each was warm and receptive to me. The lavishly furnished rooms one after the other took my breath away. No wonder there was a Revolution! If this were the "Lower House" of Parliament what might their Senate have looked like?!

Shortly after I arrived at the Grand Hall, the doors swung open on the far end and as the entourage proceeded forward, the gathering crowd parted like the Red Sea. I knew just from the presence of the man in the center that he was someone important but I honestly didn't know who he was. Still, I had been in Paris long enough to know how to punt my way through situations. The good-looking Frenchman stopped two feet from me, cameras and lights shadowing him. When he turned around to me I smiled, held out my friendly American hand and stepped forward. He and I chatted for almost five minutes trying to find either the correct English word (on his side) or the correct French word (on my side) to converse. He was about as bad with English as I was French but charming and gracious, nonetheless. He told me he had just been to the G-20 summit in Pittsburgh. We each stumbled through our conversation with humor. I apologized for my appearance, typically American tourist with sneakers (oh gads, was I sorry I wore those sneakers!) and he reassured me he understood I would be walking to buildings and museums all day.

I asked a French tourist if he would take a photo with my camera and he did. Miraculously, the photo turned out great; both of us looked quite compatible, I thought. Unfortunately, I found out later that this handsome fellow was married. Bummer.

I walked away delighted with myself but still not knowing who the heck this person was. At the door, I showed my photo to a French guard and asked him who the man was. "But!" he exclaimed, "that is the President, the President of Assemble Nationale! You are most fortunate, madam!" He seemed astonished and impressed that I had a photo of the President and myself. I scribbled down the name of *Bernard Accoyer* and impressed all my French friends with the photo. For two more hectic days I bounced around Paris taking in as many freebees as I could.

From July 21 for four weeks there were artificial beaches in Paris. It was called Paris Plages (beaches). The public looked forward to this event every year. It was loaded with activities, particularly, for families. One was located along three kilometers of the Seine. Adjacent thoroughfares closed down and people meandered, rollerbladed and otherwise enjoyed the scenery. Tons of sand was deposited in both of two or three locations. There were concert stages, clowns, Tai Chi classes, refreshments, and a temporary, large outdoor pool for the children.

Near my apartment in the nineteenth, at Bassin de la Villette, there was kayaking, beach volley ball, dancing, trampolines, big, inflatable cylinders that the children roll around in on top of the canal and arts and crafts for the kiddies. It gave the over-heated residents something that offered a little relief during those blistering summer days in Paris. I met my friends, Paul and Claire from London at the Plages and then, after Claire and I tried Tai Chi near the Seine with other Parisiennes, we sauntered over to a nearby café and had lunch.

These well-planned celebrations in Paris are always one of the exciting, sweet charms of a city I will always love (in spite of the weather).

These outdoor events are usually free. But, if you want tickets to an *indoor* event plan ahead of time! I know because I didn't! In between cloudy skies and inclement weather I managed to get to Opera Garnier three times for opera tickets each time to wait in long queues and then be told to return the next day. When I couldn't get any available opera seat, I, in my ultimate wisdom, went to Craig's List and found an Opera Ticket for the last night of an opera I had never heard: *Les Contes d'Hoffmann.* It wasn't on my wish list but I always remain open. It was playing at Opera Bastille, which was only one train ride from my apartment. I had the nerve to actually negotiate the price and ended up paying only 69 euros for a first balcony seat.

I don't like Opera Bastille. Never have. It is starkly plain, almost devoid of design, and has steep inside steps that threaten impending falls; it is, what you might call, a "rough diamond" compared to Opera Garnier. Yet, every time I have seen an Opera at Bastille, the ensemble cast has been fabulous. Whether or not it is in French, Italian or German I find the cast pulls me into the story line with the sheer force of their talent. It amazed me as they changed from one elaborate, magnificent setting to another with dozens and dozens of cast members. It was three and one-half hours of bliss for only sixty-nine euro and no queues; I had won the lottery!

Back to Craig's List I went. Craig and I were buddies by this time. If Craig were in Paris and named Pierre we might have been lovers. I found another treasure: one ticket, 6th row to Baryshnikov! Yep, the grand old master is still performing. Years ago I had paid hundreds of dollars for a ticket. Now I found one for a mere 45 euro. In this June program he was dancing with another aging ballet dancer, Anna Laguna, who actually took top billing (must have been an ego buster for Misha). It was a short program of four modern dance numbers. In one charming number he danced with a film image of his younger self. It was a glorious, thrilling, really, to feel the love for him in that audience. They overflowed with applause and appreciation. I felt so grateful to have found the ticket.

Paris hadn't improved the queue mentality in my absence, though. Everywhere there were queues. At the grocery store one would wait in line in the bakery section for those items and pay there. Want toiletries? Queue and pay in another line. Want groceries? Yep, still another line. It was all so poorly organized. I exhaled, held my tongue and remembered my French friends telling me to "embrace" the cultural differences. Yeah, right..

I couldn't take the lines at Musee d'Orsay. I just couldn't take it any more. Rain or shine, hours of queues every day suggested this was one of the world's favorite tourist meccas. So, I bought a membership, which clearly I should have bought months earlier in the fall. Now I had a special door I went through after standing in line (yep) with the other members who were also trying to avoid the hours of queues ever present in the longer, non-member lines. Are you following me?

Musee d'Orsay offered a beastly exhibit called *Crime and Punishment.* In the middle of viewing all those morbid paintings I started to giggle. All I could think of was that the audiences who attended and *admired* that exhibit were scarier than the exhibit. Why would any human being want to see paintings of mothers chopping up their children? Gross! But for me, *free,* because I was a valued member. Such a deal! Lucky me, I giggled, as all around me eyebrows raised.

Another wonderful benefit of being a member at Musee d'Orsay was that they gave you a free affiliate membership to L'Orangerie, one of my favorite museums in Paris. I ventured over there one horribly hot day to luck out: No lines! Air conditioning! Free! It was all miraculous. I stayed in that cool environment for three hours just appreciating the talents of those obsessed, prolific painters as never before (and grateful for being inside a cool place). WOW!

I ran to Le Halles Shopping Mall to purchase tickets for the Turner exhibit coming into town (more queues, of course). Eventually, it arrived, and I, smug in my knowledge of having a ticket, did not worry about queues. What bliss! Ah…well, maybe not. While there were long queues at the Grand Palais to see Turner's works, there was also a queue for those who had already purchased their tickets (you know, the ones who purchased ahead of time so they could avoid the queue?). In the heat of midday, without air conditioning, of course, massive crowds pushed and stumbled their way around each other. I can't say it made me want to linger in appreciation of this genius' art. This is the cost of the ever-popular Paris. Accept it. Embrace it. It is one of the "charms" of Paris.

While I was at Les Halles, I picked up a couple of other tickets, as well. One was to a Russian ballet in Versailles and the other to the opera "Carmen" at Chateau Vincennes. A strange thing about Paris is that the metro system doesn't coordinate scheduling with the venues offering these wonderful events. So, when I went to see "Carmen" at the end of the east metro line of Paris I knew I would have to leave before it ended. Another Bummer! I had recently found this beautiful, old Chateau Vincennes at the East end of Paris. Sitting outdoors, watching a spectacular sunset as the performance began I forgave every idiotic French advisor working in the dysfunctional Transit Department for necessitating my early leave. It was just too beautiful a moment to harbor negative sentiments towards the lack of coordination between these events and the too-early-ending metro. Still, having to leave prematurely from an important event is truly frustrating.

This early departure happened again and again, another time when I went to Versailles to the Russian ballet, also outdoors at the Neptune basin. To connect with the Paris metro before it stopped running I had to take the last train out of Versailles, which just barely connected to the last Paris train leaving for my arrondissement. That necessitated my early departure from the ballet, as well. Paris is massively populated; people need to get around at all times. It is unreasonable to expect everyone to be tucked in bed by 1 am. It is a tourist town and tourists usually don't drive in Paris. There are also very few taxis for such a highly populated city, if you can believe that. This put a real damper on attending a lot of events.

Towards the end of my visit, I was told not to miss the Yves St Laurent exhibit at the Petit Palais and I was appreciative for the good advice. Again, a ticketed event but on the beautiful weather-wise day that I attended there weren't, fortunately, as many spectators as usual. Perhaps, they were all on the streets singing and praising the return of the Good Weather God.

Some museums allow photography without flash. Others don't allow anything. As I winded my way through years of retrospective fashion I would take a quick, non-flash photo and then plunk my camera back into my purse. I had become quite covert, I thought, proudly. Really, the further into the exhibit I went the better, more extravagant and outrageous the fashions became. Click. Click. Cli—then the Security Gestapo Lady found me. Whoa! Look out. She yelled, actually, *yelled* across the room to me and all eyes followed. I admit it was a little embarrassing. She wanted to delete the photos from my camera and demanded the camera! Nasty woman! By this time, I have learned how to handle these unreasonable French people. I let her yell at me. I stood listening to her make a fool of herself, and then, like a pretty good imitation of a French person, I explained quietly I was unaware of the rule. No, I wouldn't give her my camera, which by now I had put safely in my purse. I thanked her quietly, turned and went on to see the rest of the exhibit. She had been "handled" and she knew it as she glared at me sauntering from exhibit to exhibit. I was so proud! What did they think I was going to do, for Pete's sake: Steal the designs and start my own line? This was just *retro* (albeit *fabulous* retro) *fashion*. Take a look at me, I wanted to say. Do I remotely look like a fashion designer?

Somewhere, I had heard that a new ballet was coming to Opera Garnier and pulled a friend along to keep me company. It was the morning of the sale and it would be sold out by noon most likely and I hustled him over with me. I was absolutely thrilled with my sixth row center orchestra seat to *La Petite Danseuse de Degas* to be performed at Opera Garnier. It would be the last concert of my trip, scheduled just before I left. My last splurge (I keep saying that, don't I?).

One place I went to that *didn't have a queue*, probably because it is so unknown, was the Baccarat Crystal "Museum", near Place Marlene Dietrich in the sixteenth arrondissement. Talk about elegance! Omigosh, we don't have anything like this in the U.S. that is for sure. Tiny, dazzling lights lined the wide, winding red-carpeted stairwell on both sides, leading up to the "museum", showroom and restaurant. In hushed tones, a greeter welcomes you. Everywhere there were gorgeous hanging chandeliers, sparkling, perfect table wear and jewelry. Two of the rooms reminded me of Opera Garnier with recessed ceilings, hand painted ceiling murals, exquisite gold relief statues: opulence, opulence, opulence. *How would I ever wear jeans again?* It was almost like walking into a Chocolate Factory for me: overpowering. Of course, as I would in a chocolate factory, I succumbed to the temptation of a purchase, but this time, instead of chocolate, I bought a lovely, small vase: my first Baccarat! It was a WOW place and experience.

Every now and then, intermingling with hot, humid, rainy weather there appeared a lovely, breezy day and the masses would be out in seconds wandering the streets, going on errands, meeting friends and getting exercise. It was a tease. A few hours later, gray clouds would line the sky and in seconds rained poured down upon all those souls scurrying about.

My sister had visited in the perfect October weather, one of my daughters in November (although she was sick half her visit, unfortunately). But nothing could dampen my mood because in a few days my son would be visiting me for two weeks. I was very excited. This had been a long time in the planning and I was eager to share my favorite city with him. But I was about to endure the fickle finger of fate: the corporate structure of unreasonable airline travel regulations (you know which finger that is).

Twenty Six

Within every mother's heart there is a special and deep place, a place that is filled only with love for her children. Regardless of what our children turn out to be, we mothers would fight the world like lionesses to protect our cubs. The pick of my litter is my youngest one, Brian. He has always been the sweetest, kindest, most thoughtful and sensitive of my children. Sans a few horrible high school years, we have had a healthy relationship all of his life.

At the age of thirteen Brian was diagnosed with Epilepsy. It would be a long, arduous high wire act we would navigate in the next sixteen years, fraught with many challenges along that path: paternal estrangement, the diagnosis itself, horrific medicines and their various side effects, endless doctor visits, hospital stays, unsuccessful brain surgery, depression and a Vagus nerve implant. It bonded us in a way that only mothers with ill children can understand.

So, it seemed only natural that I decided to share my favorite city in the world with Brian. As always, I would try to balance the "slings and arrows of outrageous fortune" with a trip he would never forget. Since he hoped to become a professional photographer I reasoned that this would be a lifetime opportunity to photograph one of the most beautiful cities in the world!

In January, a full five months before his intended departure, I booked our individual tickets to Paris. But I made a mistake and one I will never repeat. In an effort to cooperate with the airline industry I told Americain Airlines he sometimes had seizures. Airlines are so skittish about everything these days; I didn't want a potential seizure to be misinterpreted as aggression by the air marshals. This declaration was solely a courtesy to Americain Airlines. For my cooperation I presumed their cooperation would be reciprocated. How wrong could I get?

Americain told me they would have someone call me to find out about his condition. I waited one month and then I called them. They told me not to worry, that someone would be in touch. I waited another month and called them again to be told the same thing.

"Well", I replied, "if they wait too long I will be in Paris. I am leaving before he does, remember."

"They will see that on your tickets. Don't worry about it, ma'am." So I didn't.

Through a series of errors on Americain's part I asked Brian from Paris a few days before his flight, to contact Americain. He did and all hell broke loose.

There is such a thing as the American with Disabilities Act, which prohibits discrimination to the disabled. Now, however, airlines are bending over backwards to insure "safety" in the air. I can accept safety regulations. No problem. But the term "safety" seems to be a veil of excuses by Americain. Those excuses should not preclude, however, honoring the civil rights of our disabled. Americain had totally dropped the ball. They had planned on letting him just show up for the flight and were then going to deny access to it! Continual calls between Paris and the Dallas headquarters ensued. For the next forty-eight hours Americain would demand Brian hurry to his neurologist office to try and meet Americain's exacting, twelfth-hour demands. Since his personal neurologist was out of town, we tried to get flight authorization from another doctor.

At first Americain said they would only deal with his regular doctor. Then, we got them to accept a new doctor's assessment but were then told that wouldn't be enough. It was the night before his flight and Americain told us the doctor, who had faxed them a written authorization for flying, now had to *speak* to their department and to Americain's doctor, as well. Of course, that was impossible to coordinate with the time difference. After putting us all through hell for two days we were told he still would not be able to board the flight because it took *four* days to order oxygen (Apparently, they couldn't tell us that at the beginning!). It was a ridiculous overkill by the airlines. They had known their four-day "rule" for oxygen from the start of the entire mess.

Basically, they said "We don't want your son on our flight. It is very simple. We are canceling his ticket and will return your money. If you want to rebook and order the oxygen then you will have to pay the up charges for booking at the last moment." There was no empathy, no compassion, only attitude coming at us like fierce bull. They had had a full five months to question his condition and now denied any responsibility to us.

If you know anything about Epilepsy, you may know that seizures are exasperated by stress. It was a painful, stressful, frustrating and unfair outcome.

I was damned if this was going to keep him from his dream trip. I booked him on another airline without notification of his condition and four days later, *without oxygen* (which he had never needed, anyway) he arrived, tired but happy to see Mom waiting for him at the gate.

I am a Type A personality, goal-oriented and I was ready to lay the world of Paris at his feet. I quickly had to adjust that planned packed schedule. Here, clearly, was a frail, young man. Brian just wasn't use to any type of crammed scheduling of activities. I cut in half the schedule I had planned. Of course, as an adult he wanted to go off on his own, which unnerved me to no end. But I couldn't baby him forever.

A friend suggested once to me that all mothers worry about their children; that may well be but mothers of adult children with Epilepsy have an extra dimension of worry. With some trepidation I waved au revoir and watched him traipse off on his own exploration, praying he wouldn't have a seizure and fall on to the metro tracks or be hit by a car while crossing a rue. The humid, hot weather didn't help, either. He often decided to stay at home in the evenings watching DVDs on the television and, as he put it, "chillin' out".

It was a challenge for both of us. Brian didn't want me to worry and I, of course, worried and tried to hide it from him.

We did have fun, though. I took him to St. Chapelle's classical concert and to several fun places. We climbed up to the basilica in Montmartre and took photos at Notre Dame. We walked the 3rd, 4th, 5th, 6th arrondissements. We traveled out to Giverney to photograph Monet's gardens and had a delightful lunch there (but only after a minor seizure).

I had taken my sister to an historic restaurant, Au Vieux Paris d'Arcole, the previous October in Paris. Frankly, when I had stumbled upon it I just stood in front admiring its beauty. Built in 1512 it is one of the fortunate few ancient buildings that architect and city planner, Haussmann, did not demolish. The quaint façade had vines running up the building, with flowers dripping over the tiny sidewalk near its three outdoor tables, immediately adjacent to the narrow street. It almost didn't look real, a sort of miniature Hollywood setting. The inside had been decorated with French period furniture and I looked forward to sharing a special evening with my sis. But the service was non existent and if the waiter, who I had to track down continuously, called me "Sweetie" one more time (he should be so blessed), I would have suffocated him with the cushion on which my cute American behind sat. The food was served barely warm. Any entrée served as caisson en Papillote should be served wrapped in parchment paper. My sister's dish was served wrapped in *aluminum foil*, just like at Girl Scout camp. Au Vieux Paris d'Arcole was like a beautiful woman luring you in with no substance. I wrote a letter to the owner, who invited me back as his guest. There is nothing like the lure of a free meal, is there?

Still with some trepidation I approached the restaurant this time with Brian. The location is perfect: one block from Notre Dame on an old, winding side street. They were expecting us. At first, we sat outside, a seemingly perfect Paris setting, until the birds attacked me. Then we hurried inside. The waiters were almost comedic in their personalities. Forgiving them for their bizarre behaviors was the best thing we could do. That forgiveness and a couple of glasses of vin relaxed me. It was here Brian ordered his first-time carpaccio, and sampled – *and liked* – Mom's foie gras. That started a wonderful dining experience for us both and we eventually departed, satisfied and happy. It had turned out a memorable evening, after all.

But, changing the time frames of neurological medicines after international travel can be a difficult accomplishment in a short, two-week time frame. So it was that Brian and I would be standing in an overheated, overstuffed metro train and he would suffer a seizure. Time and time again, throughout his two weeks in Paris this happened. I am so very grateful to the French who came to our aid each and every time. They showed nothing but kindness to us and I will never forget that.

Twice we tried to go to the Eiffel Tower. The first time he writhed in pain, moaned and fell, just a block from the Tower. We took the tram back home. The second time we actually made it there. I told Brian that I would wait in the long queue to buy tickets to the top, and he could walk around photographing whatever he wanted.

As I chitchatted with a pleasant Italian woman in line next to me we both noticed the Nigerian hawkers running away from the Tower. I laughed. "I bet they see the cops coming!" I declared, amused when I was right. Two cops on bicycles arrived and our eyes followed them to the center underneath the Tower where they stopped. There was a small crowd gathered around someone on the cement. Military men surrounded the crowd with rifles. My heart stopped. My eyes searched through the crowd to see who it was; I started to slowly walk closer because I wasn't sure. Quickly it became clear that Brian was on the ground and the focus of everyone's attention. I dashed madly towards the scene. The soldiers held up their rifles and pointed them directly at me, yelling at me to stop. That, of course, wouldn't deter this lioness from getting to her cub.

I yelled at them "I am his mother, his mere, his maman! Get out of my way!"

They would have to shoot me to stop me. *Even they recognized that.* They lowered their rifles as I frantically passed them, elbowing my way into the center gathered the crowd.

There on the ground, covered from head to toe in blood, was my cub. He was beginning to come out of seizure format, still dazed and incoherent. A Dutch woman and her husband had been the first to his side. She held his head to keep it from banging into the cement and her husband held Brian's expensive camera so no one would walk away with it. They were angels sent to us by God that day, that hour, that moment. There is no other explanation.

Brian didn't immediately recognize me. He looked up at me, eyes still dilated, his face, hair and clothing bloodied from biting his tongue and he couldn't speak. A noticeable pool of blood soaked into the cement next to him. I wanted to cry, to cry for this horrible neurological disorder from which he suffered so. I wanted to cry for the little, sweet boy I had brought up who didn't deserve the cards he was being dealt. I wanted to cry for his future, how challenging it would be. I wanted to cry for the loneliness he would experience when one day his greatest ally would no longer be there to protect him. But I didn't have that luxury. I had to be strong for him; he didn't need to worry about an overwrought mother, crying at his side.

When an ambulance arrived we requested The American Hospital in Paris, where I had spent eleven days years earlier when I had to have emergency surgery while visiting Paris. Instead, they sped us to a local public hospital. At first, seeing only three other people in the emergency room, I thought we might get through to a doctor fairly quickly. Wrong again. I walked around the check-in station to find people in gurneys lining a long corridor, waiting to see a doctor. This is the practicality of socialized medicine in Paris at least at public hospitals.

I told the nurse I wanted to get a cab and take Brian home. He had forgotten to take his meds that morning and that is what he needed now. That and rest. I was informed that if an ambulance brings someone in they were not allowed *by law* to release the patient prior to seeing the doctor.

"Let me put it this way" I glowered, "If you make us wait six or eight hours he will be that much sicker. You and your hospital will be liable. If you call us a cab I can have him home with his meds and resting in less than an hour." Don't mess with me, sister, I glared at her. Apparently, everyone recognizes an agitated lioness when they see one. She backed off, suddenly seeing the reasonableness of my request and called a cab. Off we were skirted to the far side of the city away from hospitals, doctors, blood, rifles and crowds. It was a good decision. He would recover and resume his holiday the next morning.

It was with great relief that I eventually waived goodbye to my little cub at the airport. I had gotten Brian through his Parisian experience in one piece. I had shared with him something I believe he will always remember.

I exhaled long and hard. I needed *balance*! I needed N.O.

Good Lord, was I ready for some fun!

Twenty-Seven

I continued meeting gentlemen who had patiently waited for my son's departure. Through Meetig I was contacted by Hady, my first and only Muslim man. He had been born in Morocco, lived in Paris for decades and he spoke proficient English, as well. After exchanging emails, we talked on the phone.

Morocco triggered memories for me. I had actually been to Morocco (a hundred years earlier) with an attractive American I had met at the bullfights in Malaga, Spain, just across the straight of Gibraltar. We spent the day in Tangiers exploring the tiny alleyways and district areas with their snake "charmers" and veiled women. It was a fun, exotic experience, as I recalled. Well, *most* of it was.

You have to recognize that when I was twenty-one and traveling I was an innocent young girl. *Yes I was*! There was no trail of betraying men, few liars and I was, well, I was virginal *thinking*. My companion's name was Jack and he asked me to hide a stash of hashish for him when we hydra-foiled back across the border to Spain. I never did marijuana. I just wasn't interested. I wasn't exactly sure of what hashish was. I had traveled through many European countries on my own. I had such a fresh, clean appearance that I was never stopped at any border for a baggage check as so many my age were (it was, after all, the sixties!). So I stuck it in my hat and thought nothing of it. I really didn't know enough about it to worry.

That day, however, the guards were out searching for it. They inspected every bag I had, poured through the contents, even, embarrassingly, the tampons, looking for an illegal substance. The dogs were not far off. As this scenario progressed, I noticed Jack slowly inching away from me. Clearly, he was distancing himself from the scene and disassociating himself with me. My heart sank. What would happen if they asked for my hat, I wondered. The search continued and Jack left me standing there alone. Finally, after much ado, they waved me through, never having checked my hat. What would have happened had they thought of looking under the young girl's hat? I could still be languishing away in some Moroccan prison without rights, without privacy, without nutrition, being raped by prison guards and, basically, rotting away. I still shutter when I think of it. As I look back at that young girl, I want to shake her. "Wake up! Be careful!" Now I do it with the old girl.

Hady took me out to an enchanting French café, Café Louis Phillipp, dated from 1810, on the right bank of the Seine not far from Pont Marie, the eastern corner of the 4th arrondissement. Johnny Depp had filmed a scene there; unfortunately, the huba huba hunk wasn't there when we were. I was the only English-speaking person there. Hadi spoke fluent French and handled everything for us. We had a gloriously wonderful dejeuner (lunch). We started with white wine and appetizers then progressed to rouge. I wondered how all this excessive wine consumption effected productivity when they returned to work, to say nothing of the expense of it all. But I didn't linger very long with that "productivity" concern; it was all such American thinking, anyway.

I was fascinated with this, my first introduction to Muslim men. Of course, Modern western Muslim men don't dress in anything that bespoke of religious garb. They really enjoyed all the benefits of modern society.

"I am a man of peace!" Hady declared, as I tried to query him on his religious views. That was that; he really didn't want to talk about it. I was disappointed; I had hoped to learn more about his customs and religion but it was obvious he didn't want to share.

Hady recommended the duck with morel sauce and I salivated over this tasty, succulent selection for a long time. Then he insisted on a fromage course. Far be it for me to be rude; I happily accepted the plate of cheeses and we lingered over this as we polished a bottle of red wine. It was a perfect, sunny, breezy day in Paris and I couldn't have been more content (good wine, food and weather were a sure combination that always equated to happiness). We were the last customers out of the café, satisfied, a little tipsy (at least I was) and very content.

Hady insisted on driving me home, which I initially thought was most thoughtful. *Initially*. When will I ever learn? I was ready to jump out at the curb of my apartment building but instead he parked the car.

"Surely, you want to extend hospitality to me?"

Duh, I hadn't planned too. My guard was down (*of course, it was down after all that wine!*) so up the elevator we rode to my apartment. I went to the kitchen to get us some ice tea and before I knew it he was right behind me, nuzzling my neck. I turned around to face him. Before I could say anything, good, old Hady wasted no time waiting to kiss me.

"I must make a note of this", I thought to myself. "Never invite anyone up to the apartment after a bottle and half of wine". But somehow that was only a passing caution. Hady was all over me. So much for his strict Muslim faith. He had the strangest way of kissing me. If I had categorized his kissing in my previous kissing chapter I would have called him "The-Chicken-With-the-Head-Cut-Off" Kisser. His tongue darted wildly around in my mouth. If I hadn't had so much to drink, I would have started to laugh. He conclusively was an inducted member of the International Kissing Hall of Shame, that was for sure. What was he thinking? Wasn't it time for my good Muslim friend to pray or something? Which direction was Mecca?

I have found a quiet amusement in this my independent survey of kissing men. Who teaches us all how to kiss, anyway? Did some Moroccan lady, high on hashish, teach him this "style"? If he was this energetic *after* a bottle and half of wine what would he be like *before?*

A man of "peace"? *Maybe I had misspelled the word.* I managed to quickly escort my Moroccan ami to the door. He promised to call. I fell into bed, exhausted from it all. What a crazy day, I thought, as I fell asleep.

Hady did call. We planned to go to an art exhibit of one of his favorite artists: Takeshi Kitano, a Japanese actor, painter, television personality and celebrity-at-large. I had never heard of him before, which frustrated my escort. It wasn't my type of art, as it turned out but I do recognize this artist had talent. The paintings and exhibits were very modern and colorful with a bit of Picasso influence in some of them. It is not an exhibit I would have attended if Hady hadn't invited me. Still, if I am to consider myself an art buff I must remain open to all types of art; so I found this another interesting excursion and tried my best to respond to Hady's enthusiasm for his artist.

Afterwards, we went to lunch in my old neighborhood, the fifteenth. Again, the wine flowed, the food was good and our conversation lively. As we walked our way back to the car I went to hold his hand and he pulled away and off he huffed. Literally. He hurried ahead of me like I had the plague. Had my spastic Headless Chicken lost interest? I think it had something to do with his Muslim background. Hady didn't express public displays of affection. It was a little weird considering how aggressive he became behind closed doors. By the time we got into the car, I was in a huff, rejected by The-Chicken-With-His-Head-Cut-Off Kisser. But not for long.

He started the engine and turned to me with his hand on my thigh. Opps! I was not rejected but I didn't like this policy of no PDA; this behind-the-doors policy was hypocritical. Calmly, I removed his hand from my leg and looked out the side window. Of course, he didn't like that at all. We drove over towards Notre Dame and he pulled the car to the side of the road.

"Did you have a good time?" he asked, coolly. I nodded.

"I think we were not meant to be." *No kidding*, I thought.

"You need to get out of here and do what you want…" Truthfully, I agreed but I had never in my whole life been dumped on a corner before. I didn't know whether to laugh or get angry. I laughed.

"Au revoir!" I smiled and waved as I slammed the car door closed. At least I didn't have to worry about another attempted seduction at my apartment. It was a beautiful afternoon and I meandered around Paris appreciative of the international experience and nonetheless for wear.

I decided to accept a Meet Up invitation to a social engagement in the fifth. It was there I met Patrick, who I affectionately dubbed My Cave Man. He knew it, too. He had been called that before. Patrick was the United Nations. French born but with ties all over the world, he had traveled to all the corners of the globe. Very educated, he taught university classes in Political Science and Modern World Economics. He lectured to graduate students and the public. He worked for years as a journalist and still traveled to such exotic places as Afghanistan, Pakistan and Iraq. He spoke seven languages and had five wives not all at the same time, of course. Still, his appearance was that of a Cave Man. He had messy blond hair, which looked dyed but he vowed was not. He had a scraggy beard. His clothing generally was, how shall I put this delicately….Cave Man Chic! He had a low, gravely voice but twinkling, intelligent eyes. One could easily imagine him trekking the mountains of Afghanistan undetected but *Paris*? Still, he lived in the center of

Paris. He was the most unusual man I have ever met and I will say this for him: as he noticed me appearing in fashionable attire he rived up his fashion wardrobe, which I appreciated enormously.

We became friends. I just couldn't imagine more. While he seemed interested in me he took my queue and never made a move on me. It allowed me to relax and just enjoy the man of the world that he was. He knew every unusual, international dinning spot in Paris and we frequented those at my request or his suggestion. He remained a gentleman throughout my stay and I considered him a friend although not someone who actually would fit into my every day life. I think he knew and accepted that. He may have felt the same way.

Georges contacted me through Meetig. He asked me out to dinner and drinks. Off I went. Georges considered himself an upper crust type of fellow, complete with affectation, particularly with his tone of English. Retired, he had recently returned to work because, as he put it, "it was just too good of a deal to pass". He had that pretentious air about him that doesn't promote Franco-American good will. So impressed with himself, he actually proudly opened his jacket to show me the "Hugo" label inside. Lord, I thought, if he is trying to impress women with a label there can't be much depth to him.

As soon as he met me he told me he had to go back to work after our wine. Now, to a new woman that means one of two things: his first impression of the woman (that would be me) isn't good enough to spend time and euro on dinner or he did actually have to go back to work but wasn't thoughtful enough to call me ahead of time. Either way, it is an awkward way of beginning a meet. Either way, whether he was interested or not, he wasn't my cup of tea. We drank our aperitif and then he walked me over to the metro assuming I was going directly home. But he had a surprise for me.

We looked at the metro map together and before I knew it he turned into a frog! *Really*. Apparently, I was the fly. His long tongue protruded out of his mouth for what appeared about twenty-four inches. I do not exaggerate. I think it was the longest tongue I have ever seen. I stood there, stunned, mesmerized by the frog's tongue (Is that how flies feel right before they are eaten?). He didn't wait till our mouths met; he literally thought he could lure me in as a frog does to a fly by jetting his tongue out and then pulling me into it. He kept doing it. I didn't want to make a scene but honestly, now, I wish I had slapped his face. File this guy under Frog Kisser. Yuck! Another Member in Good Standing of the International Kissing Hall of Shame.

When I told My Cave Man about it, he wrinkled his nose in disgust and thought it was as gross as I did. "Stop!" My Cave Man pleaded. He didn't want to hear any more. But I thought it was very funny and laughed later that Cave Man and I were simpatico. What we women have to go through for a good kiss! Gads!

I had been SKYPEing for weeks with a German man (I should have been forewarned; remember Adolph!) who met me through Meetig. I love the SKYPE system of communication because you can actually see the person as you talk to them through your computer. I used it all the time and it was *free*. His name was Alf, which he told me meant "noble wolf". Hmmm. Was that supposed to impress me? What is noble about a wolf, anyway?

Alf decided to fly to Paris to meet me. Of course, I dolled myself up and went to our meeting place to wait an hour for what turned out to be a no-show. Nothing pisses me off more than being stood up, especially after I go to some trouble to actually make myself more presentable. This takes longer than it used to, as you can imagine, since I am now sixty-four whopping years young.

Alf called the next day explaining, without apology, he apparently went to the wrong place. Obviously, I thought, still rattled. Eventually, we did meet behind Notre Dame ((I should have insisted on the Eiffel Tower since it always attracted better karma for me). It was a hot day and I didn't really want to walk but he did. German men decide everything. So we walked over the walk bridge to Ile St Louis, an island across a walk bridge from Notre Dame on that sweltering hot day.

We ended up in what appeared to be a quaint restaurant, although we were the only ones there (not a good sign). No wine, Alf declared. He didn't drink during the day and didn't ask me if I wanted a glass. The best thing I can say for the restaurant is that it was pretty and we had a friendly waiter. The food was very average. Of course, there would be no dessert or fromage with my frugal Dutchman.

But what really bothered me was that he immediately started talking about how the American servicemen mistreated the French people right after the Liberation.

"Their behavior was despicable!" Alf declared, challenging me. I looked at him like he was crazy. Finally, after listening to this crap for a long time, I turned to him and said: "Considering how the Germans behaved to the Jews I can't imagine how you can criticize the Americans who liberated France!" I wished I had said it earlier in the conversation. I see no reason to be endlessly polite to a man who is being rude.

After lunch, in the heat of day, old Alf wanted to walk some more. It simply was too hot to walk and I told him so. Irked, he watched me go to my metro, biding him an Auf Wiedersehen. Good riddance to my "noble wolf". I exhaled with gratitude as I made my escape.

There are "the players" on websites like Meetig and Catch.com. They simply use it as sport. But the Frenchmen could be amusing even hilarious. One, Christophe-Henri, was in constant communiqué with me. He called me his "Queen", sent me flowery emails constantly, yet every time we talked about getting together he backed off with one excuse or the other. There was a fine balance between amusement and wasting my valuable time. But still, as I tell you my story, he emails me and calls me his "Queen", the love of his life, the one he truly holds in his heart. It was all hysterical rubbish.

Ah, yes, this was an international experience, alright. But it did set up a deep appreciation for the good and more interesting men I had yet to meet.

In between all this arrived an email. It was from Jules who remembered I had planned to come back to Paris for the summer. He asked to call me and I agreed. I really wasn't sure how I felt about Jules other than residual aggravation from his last departure. Eventually, he arrived at my apartment, an hour late.

When I attempted to broach the November incident he refused to talk about it. He had survived an overbearing, impossible father who dominated with negativity. Jules, as a result, hated any confrontation even though it may be well deserved (this, I am sure, will cause many problems for him in the future). A man cannot just leave a relationship without explanation and then attempt to reenter it.

He assumed too much. Frankly, he was too aggressive for me. I didn't like it. It didn't feel comfortable. We women carry our bruises around, don't we? They don't just evaporate. Unless there is a frank conversation about how to avoid whatever happened that lack of resolution prohibits us from going forward with any deal of forgiveness or grace.

Jules came over once more and still didn't want to talk about November. So I showed him the door. He contacted me a couple of other times via email and I passed up on it as those invitations came, as always, too late. Some things never change.

We had had our moment. I was content to let him go. This time, au revoir was not hard to say.

Still, there was more to my life than this…

Twenty Eight

Because Paris is such a densely populated city with millions of residents, tourists, students and temporary occupants crammed into tall apartment buildings one next to the other, it becomes a city one must escape from upon occasion. Those escapes are normally centered around religious holidays that provide elongated weekends. In the summer, however, everyone in Paris wants to elude the heat with regular sojourns to the seaside or the hills and valleys of France. I would be no different.

I had been taking regular day trips to my favorite place, Versailles. There is so much to Versailles in, around and beyond the gardens with their spectacular fountains. Versailles offers regular concerts, fireworks, and ballets. I loved to meander around Marie Antoinette's Estates with its lovely landscaping and photo opportunities. My favorite thing, however, was to just rent a bicycle at the Palace grounds and venture out to the surrounding forests. I was blessed on several occasions with perfect weather (It always seemed cooler in Versailles), encouraging me on kilometer after kilometer. Scenic roads morphed into beautiful trails that winded into paths that were totally isolated from the crowds in the Gardens. There was also a bike path that wound for miles around the cross-shaped Grand Canal where kings used to fish. On and on I peddled, breeze ruffling through my hair, singly like Julie Andrews in "The Sound of Music", deliriously happy just being alone in pure bliss. When I found such peace, such happiness it served as a poignant reminder that some of my more precious moments have been spent on my own, without "international" experience or men. They were moments of pure joy in just being alive. *Joie le vivre*.

I had always wanted to see the city of Chartres, another lengthier day trip. I was completely enthralled with the surprise of how much I enjoyed this sweet, picturesque little town a few hours southwest of Paris. But I hadn't paid close enough attention on the train, missed my stop and rambled on to the end of the line. Then I had to wait till a return train came and brought me back to where I was supposed to be. All of that was a colossal waste of time. Had I known I would enjoy the town so much I would have made reservations to stay over-night.

The Cathedral of Notre Dame, of course, is why pilgrims have ventured to Chartres for a thousand years. Chartres' Cathedral is considered one of the best examples in the world of Gothic Cathedrals. It has some of the World's largest, most amazing medieval stained glass windows, which both thrilled and irritated me. The windows were constructed to capture the light of the sun, symbolic of the Light of God and to give the people something to see because religious services took place far from their view at the front of the Cathedral. The windows were constructed so high it is nearly impossible to fully appreciate the details without binoculars. How, then, were pilgrims a thousand years ago, able to fully absorb the biblical scenes depicted there? Still, it is a breathtaking excursion into a precious time in history. I actually wanted to go back and reread the voluminous "Pillars of the Earth" for a refresher course on what workmen endured to build these spectacular homages to Mary, Mother of Jesus.

Little cobbled streets and alleys surround the Cathedral and street signs belie what happened here a thousand years ago; one tiny street, rue des Changes was where visitors needed to exchange money. Another, rue Lait, sold milk, another Herbes, or Cheese or Fish. Each street retained its original, directional names from more than a thousand years ago.

I loved it all and hope to return one day for a longer stay.

I had previously traveled over most of France so for a cultural change I decided to visit Bruges, Belgium, which had been highly recommended to me. Bruges is located at the north end of Belgium near the North Sea. The whole historic centre is a UNESCO World Heritage site. I could see why.

When the bus delivered me to the city's center I found myself smiling ear to ear. It also was a city that dates back to medieval times with streets and alleys and quaint canals and parks but with the added dimension of being the *cleanest* small city I have ever visited. Even with the endless horse-drawn carriages (and the residuals that fell from the horses) that promenaded the tourists around town they somehow manage to keep it in pristine condition.

The Square is surrounded with historic buildings from a variety of centuries dating back seven centuries, fascinating in itself. Throughout this medieval city were endless cafes where tourists can sit and enjoy the music and festivals and bicyclists circulating around the Square. The museums, Flemish art galleries, endless shopping opportunities and aromatic chocolatiers make this a lively, happy city.

I happened to be there on one of their many scheduled musical festivals. At the far end of the Square was a huge stage. In the evening everyone gathered for dancing, drinking, singing and swaying back and forth to the music. I stood in the middle of the crowd joining them in camaraderie of spirit, listening to some of their Dutch favorites and many renditions of artists I knew: Tom Jones, Dolly Parton, Elvis, and Michael Jackson. It was all great fun in an engaging, historic city. For a short time I was actually able to forget the hot spell that was apparently not being experienced in just Paris but throughout Europe that summer.

There was a difference between the people of Bruges and of Paris. Except for a couple of surly waiters (who were probably imports from Paris), the people were more easy-going, hospitable and genteel. Even watching their fresh-faced young people was an interesting comparison; they were cleaner, better attired and when they kissed each other they were short, sweet, innocent kisses. It was more religious, too. There were statues of the Blessed Mother above doors everywhere and the feel of spirituality was prevalent.

On several acres, there was a Beguinage (rows of white houses built in 1235) where the cloistered nuns lived and took care of the senior residents. This reminded me that I did not see one beggar in Bruges, not one! There were endless canals that I biked along, getting lost along the way. There were beautiful parks, particularly Minnewater, where I picnicked and rested under the shade of endless trees, near its hills and winding ponds. Overall, I sensed a spirit there that transcends the people, the history, the buildings, and the centuries. There was an impression of peace and tranquility and once you get out of the commercial areas, it was meditative.

That is to say little of the limitless chocolatiers who tempted me every moment of every day (a blessing and a curse). I ate enough to get sick on the way back to Paris. Yeah, I know: *Lead Us Not Into Temptation*. I do that very well myself.

Finally, I would be remiss not to tell you about my hiking group in Paris, which led to many wonderful day trips in and around Paris.

On my eighth trip to Paris I found a hiking group associated with a continuing education facility. I signed up. There were several things I loved about the group. Firstly, I saw parts of Paris and its' surrounding areas as I never would have were it not for the guidance and hospitality of this group. Every Wednesday we would meet in early morning to begin our journeys. Someone had previously planned and announced beforehand where we would be going. Usually, it was outside of Paris. One time we went to the forests surrounding Saint German en Laye, a half-hour train ride to the west. Another time we trained to Forest de Rambouillet, south of Paris. We would traipse around all day, stopping for lunch in the forest and then forge onward. I admired this hearty group of people for their rigorous dedication to walking long distance. The French participants, most of whom spoke English, had been doing this for up to twenty years. The English-speaking folks generally spoke good French. It was an extraordinary way to meet French people.

In July I volunteered to lead the group through the parks and canal of the nineteenth arrondissement. Newcomers rarely led but I was happy to share the little I did know, as a way of relieving their normal leaders for a week. I asked the Yanks to bring something for everyone that they would have had at a July 4 picnic, and I asked the French to wear Red, White and Blue. Some brought large American flags. (Where they ever got it or why they had them still puzzles me. Would we have huge French flags in our home?)

We trekked along St Martin canal through the many parks of the nineteenth, arriving, finally, in a park not far from my favorite, Buttes Charmont: Parc de Belleville, which I hadn't yet seen myself. It was a small, hilly park. We approached it from the top and decided to descend via the area set up for children. The average age of our group was about sixty; Heck, we were all well on our way to becoming mumbling little children, anyway, so we first tackled the children's play/treehouse letting ourselves down the ropes and ladders. Then we traversed the two-story long slides. I took loads of photos of the gleeful participants and it did more for Franco American relations than any politician I have ever heard. Afterwards, I was contacted by several members who thanked me and told me I was the only rookie volunteer they ever had and that they appreciated the fun we all enjoyed together that day.

But as you know by now there is more to my life than this…

Twenty Nine

So many men. So little time.

In between the lame dates were some very fun and interesting men. Through Meetig I met a gentleman, Oliver, from Bordeaux. He came in to spend the day with me. He was a good-looking man, blinded in one eye by a childhood firecracker. Oliver was intelligent and interested in me. *Of course he was intelligent if he was interested in me.* We walked together for hours, had lunch and bid each other farewell at the metro. I invited him to come for another visit and then I promised to come visit him in his hometown. We planned another meeting but I believe his friends discouraged him. He wrote me a sweet email explaining that perhaps his friends were right and that there would be too many cultural differences, especially the language (he spoke some English but not well) and apologized for canceling our next meeting. I was disappointed but not devastated.

Some of my favorite dates came through Craig's List. They were an interesting mix of international businessmen who traveled regularly through Paris. One American, Jess, was a dentist from Atlanta. A bit self-absorbed, he dominated most of our conversations. Still, most of what he said had great interest to me; it had to do with cuisine, travel and history, my favorite topics. And, Praise God, he sure knew how to kiss! He took me to interesting restaurant, founded in 1930 after being a cobbler's shop in the sixth: Roger la Grenouille Restaurant. Many luminaries such as Pope John XXIII have eaten here in this baroque setting with its very traditional food and warm hospitality. They specialized in frog dishes but I elected to have my favorite again, foie gras, which melted in my mouth. This is another typical, tiny French restaurant. Its' walls hung with adornments from its historic past. Little tables sandwiched couples and there was no conversation privacy but everyone, with tolerance, waived that right. The dessert was....err... us! When we departed we were feeling no pain (blame it on the wine, the ambience, the conversation). Three steps out of the restaurant Jess kissed me. Thank God: A good kisser! Then we made a spectacle of ourselves as people sauntered by admiring the older, passionate couple leaning against the shadowed building. So French.

Jess took off to a planned event in Normandy and we met again in the week, his last night, at Restaurant Chez Francis. I chose Chez Francis because of its view of the Eiffel Tower, which continued to thrill me. But even though those kisses of his were hot and heavy I found he talked *incessantly* and that began to put a damper on it all. Still, I remember him with fondness and while I elected not to take it any further, it wasn't for a lack of passion.

Another Craig's List date was Charles, a businessman from Johannesburg. Tall and handsome, he was really very dear. We got on from the start. The problem with most men you meet on Craig's List in Paris is that they are in Paris for only a short time. We went out a few times and played with our mutual attraction. But did I want to jump into bed with every traveling salesman? I think not!

Still, if I am to be honest (I have never lied to you yet, have I?) passion awaited us when Charles saw me home to the inside lobby of my apartment building. I could not invite him up because my son was upstairs (I have to learn to use that excuse more often, whether Brian is "upstairs" or not). But our farewells in that lobby were prolonged. In Paris apartment building lights just don't stay on very long. They automatically go off after a brief ten or fifteen seconds; it is, I think, supposed to save electricity. But, oh-my-goodness, how sexy that made good-byes!

We were all over each other as he pressed me against the mirrored wall, fogging it up with panting and hot breathing. We felt like we were the stars of some steamy French movie and it only made us want more. While the "Hammam" wasn't a turn on, this certainly was! There is nothing like knowing you can't "do it" to make you want to "do it" even more! Charles and I intertwined our bodies, pushing and pulling each other wanting more, teasing each other but knowing we dared not go further. Gees, I am getting hot and bothered just remembering us.

Out of the blue, or should I say darkened hallway, arrived another resident: boom! On go the lights! Hello neighbor! OK, I hid my face in Charles chest and continued holding him. The young newcomer had to be amused (he was Parisian after all). But, he was polite enough to look away and continue on leaving us to our pursuit of elevating our Nitric Oxide levels.

Bless him for that! Up, up the N.O. levels went (along with other things).

I have heard from Charles but he lives on the other side of the world. That would leave infinitesimal odds of our ever really starting something lasting. How do you say au revoir in Africaneze?

I was steadily seeing someone who became a dear friend. Andre was a born French man who lived in Paris most of his life. He had a curious combination of ethics, morals and weaknesses. He intrigued me. The first time we met under the Eiffel Tower he brought charm and dry humor. Off we went to the place des Vosges where he had booked dinner reservations. In this miniscule café again I was the only English-speaking patron. There, at our table by the window was a huge bunch of flowers, which, apparently, he had stopped to deliver prior to dinner. It took my breath away. That was typical for Andre who was an exceedingly thoughtful, kind, gentle soul.

There was something authentic about our relationship. As we each began to trust one another, we found out things that neither of us would have had the courage to tell anyone else. Andre suffered from depression. He always had a sad look on his face. But behind that sadness lie intelligence, sincerity, dry (very dry) humor and the wonderful ability to not judge anyone. It was so refreshing. I never expected him to be the love of my life nor he me. That, perhaps, is what gave our friendship wings.

One evening he stayed overnight with me. We were both a little drunk but still cognitive of what we were doing (or not doing as the case may be). Andre had listened to my female complaints about men not appreciating what kissing and touching was all about. So, he said, with a glint in his eye, he was going to "nurture" me. Hmmm, I thought. Well, no hmmm; It was one of the most memorable evenings in Paris. He had no hidden agenda but to give me pleasure. *What a noble agenda*! Andre merely grazed his fingertips over every area of my body *but* the strategic three areas that most men first gravitate to. He lightly traced my arms, my face, and my legs with his gentle fingertips, and I, feeling like a princess, fell to sleep with that gentleness that he brought to our friendship. Intimacy without sex: a real gift.

We continued to see each other till our last dinner date the Saturday before I left Paris. Up to the 54th floor of the Montparnasse Building to a modern restaurant called Le Ciel de Paris in the fourteenth arrondissement we glided in thirty-eight seconds. Montparnasse is the tallest skyscraper in France, a full fifty-nine stories high. Some believe the view to be better from here than anywhere else in Paris. We watched as the panoramic views of a slowly setting sun settled over the city and shimmering lights appeared. The Eiffel Tower twinkled brightly, not so far away. We exhaled, smiled and then turned ourselves over to the more serious adventure of perusing our menu.

First, we started with a glass of champagne. We were immediately presented with a variety of tinsy, one-bite size appetizers (the French call them "Amuse-Bouche") sent with compliments of the chef to awaken the palette. Amusement, indeed! Bienvenue to another fabulous French culinary beginning! I didn't care for the pretentiousness of our waiter but eventually my dear Andre won his favor and then service and attitude improved with each passing course.

Everything on the menu appeared extraordinarily enticing. After reading it with fervor we finally managed to decide on our favorites. I ordered a cold crab dish with parmesan chips and Andre a fantastic cold foie gras. For the entree Andre chose a Steak and I a Chicken Breast stuffed with foie gras served with a small portion of delicate angel hair pasta swimming in a divine sauce that was influenced by that foie gras (at that point I thought I saw angels outside the windows of the skyscraper…). Then, he ordered us a fromage course. If that weren't enough, Andre insisted on desserts for us and far be it from me to argue. I ordered what we Yanks call Napoleons but the French call Mille-feuille. This was the restaurant's version made with layers of puff pastry, whipped cream and served with a raspberry coulis. He had a flourless chocolate torte with ice cream.

Through this extravagant meal we sipped on a bottle of Medoc and talked about our futures. Savoring each mouthful, I didn't want this culinary experience to end. It rivaled my lunch at La Tour d'Argent the previous November. Again, I had died and gone to heaven. One final, albeit pricy ($425 US), last indulgence before I boarded the plane home.

But I remember Andre not just for these extraordinary culinary excursions but for his dear, sweet, gentle manner, his decency and honest conversation. I will always consider him a friend.

Thirty

Sandwiched between music, men and meals were some blossoming friendships with women from around the world who were either living in Paris permanently, temporarily or passing through. It was such a privilege to get to know them. They made my stay richer for having crossed their paths.

An American, Robin, shared many interests with me. She had been living in Paris for over three years when we met at a Meet Up party. She was a trained culinary professional, as I was and loved many of the same things I did - except exercise. We would jaunt off for all sorts of excursions: music, French movies, theatre, special culinary adventures and local fairs. We shared information on what was happening in Paris. We were buds, confidants, friends, amis.

When Robin called me to complain of heat exhaustion – and rightfully so – I urged her to get immediately in a cold shower and bring her body temperature down. I am sure I saved her life.

One of the reasons I chose summer was that I had never celebrated Bastille Day in Paris. Since Robin had lived in Paris much longer, she was savvy about local "happenings". She steered us both down to her neighborhood for the annual Fireman's Ball that happens the night before Bastille, their version of our Independence Day. Many of the fire stations participate in this very local merrymaking gala. We lined up (how unusual) and were admitted early after making our voluntary contribution to the Firemen's Widows Fund. That seemed fair enough. The event attracted the entire neighborhood. They had a huge band and singers on a professional stage and people drank, talked, laughed and danced to the music. Several cute, young, virile firemen gladly surrounded me for a photo. After a few hours we left. Those darn metros would prevent us from staying until the celebrations closed at 4 AM. That was fine; I had experienced a real local event and was satisfied with getting home by 1 AM. But I was constantly leaving events early, as I have shared, to accommodate the metro schedules. When do they get their act together and start running those metros *non-stop, around the clock*?!

Inclement weather permeated Paris through Bastille Day. Rain clouds gathered and sprinkled on and off preventing everyone from their rituals. We had planned a gourmet picnic in the park by the Eiffel Tower. Rain countermanded that aspiration. When all else failed, our masterminded last chance effort was to pray to the Big Guy Upstairs for a clearing in the sky so we could, at least, attend the fireworks that evening. It worked; our prayers were answered.

Down we ventured to a place near the fireworks, not far from the Eiffel Tower. I had no real raincoat in Paris so I covered myself in a large plastic garbage bag (unused, of course) in case it started to pour again. Tre chic! Again, I looked like an immigrant from the New World, as non-Parisian as I looked when I met Mehmet that first night I arrived in May. No wonder we Yanks have a bad fashion reputation! But no one cared. Everyone understood; we were all in the same wet boat together. It was great fun and everyone reveled in the fireworks, unabated by rain. Five minutes after the fireworks stopped, the rain poured down on the crowd. I had, at least, enjoyed the Bastille Day Fireworks. It was all a small, French miracle thanks to the Big Weather God Upstairs.

Another "thing" we "shared" (unbeknownst to each other at least initially) was the same man. Luke, whom I have mentioned previously, had also pursued Robin a year earlier. We figured this out after Robin and I had attended a small theatre performance together. We sat and sipped our wine and talked about (tada!) men. Imagine that. Luke was supposed to pick me up from the theatre to take me out for dinner afterwards. When I told her his name, she nearly choked on her wine. Robin warned me that he was still married, although separated from his wife who lived hundreds of miles away. Gulp! We both were curious to see how he would handle the two of us advancing arm in arm towards him. Bursting with laughter we relished the thought of pending introductions. Of all the millions of men in Paris wouldn't you know we both had gone out with the same guy? He must have busted a gut seeing us together that night as I introduced him to my friend. We thought it was hysterical. It was all craziness and having a sense of humor really helped.

Another time, after a French movie, I urged her to go to a dance place, Le Caveau De La Huchette in the Latin Quarter that I had previously been to and we hurried in, down the stairs into the basement and had a fabulous time. First, Jacques Louis approached me to dance. Now this was a place, as I have said before, where patrons were talented enough to be competitive; they were that good. Boy, did he challenge me to dance that night! Holy Schmoly! He probably was twenty-five years younger than I was but I was not going to be outdone. Damn, if but for one hour, I was my old self moving with confidence, ease, and enjoyment to the crazy, pulsating music, never missing a beat, never begging for mercy. I felt like the crazed Jules Feiffer cartoon character, The Dancer. Finally, I encouraged Jacques Louis to ask Robin to dance just so I could take a break.

Grandma was near cardiac arrest by this time. I was soaked. Sweat poured down my face and boobs. I knew the only thing that could save me was a cold shower at home. Robin isn't much of a dancer and J-L thoughtfully slowed down for *her*. But Grandma had had it. I told Robin that I was surrendering myself to an anticipated cold shower. Besides, I had to grab that last metro home before I was stuck. I urged her to persevere with old whatshisname. Maybe she would get lucky. I staggered my way to the metro and home to take a long, cold shower. Eventually, my palpitating heart calmed down and I could once more breathe. It may have been my last hurrah on the dance floor but what a hurrah!

Another time, Robin and I went to an *authentic* Hammam on Ladies' Day. We detoxed with steam, sauna, went in a freezing cold pool, had clay slathered over our bodies, fell asleep in the relaxation room and were given a wonderful massage. Weak, relaxed and revived, we staggered out the door. Time for vin!

Like we had done on the eve of my first departure we once again sought out a special restaurant, Drouant's, as a farewell meal. While I enjoyed it, there was no comparison to the thrill I had the previous November at Tour d'Argent. After a couple of glasses of vin I smiled at the three businessmen next to us and asked if they planned to, indeed, enjoy those truffles left by the waiter. Graciously, they handed over the entire plate of truffles, apparently amused with the female addiction to chocolate. *Have I told you I loved Paris?*

I met a lovely Italian woman who had lived in Paris for decades with her husband. She treated me to tea and we attended some day concerts together. Unfortunately, she traveled a great deal and I wasn't able to get to know her better. But I appreciate her openness to a new friend.

I met a funny lady from the Philippines in the Open Air Market Place who, through a date website, met and ended up marrying a French man who was crazy about her. She radiated energy to all who knew her. Our own little energizer bunny. It was she and her husband who helped me register for my free membership in the French date site, Meetig.

When I took my second tour of Notre Dame I met an English-speaking French Guide, Martine, who loved to share Paris as it gave her opportunity to practice her English. She offered to show me Paris as a guide for free. She was hardly the image of the average Parisian woman. Martine was short, unfashionable with crooked teeth but she was the nicest woman in Paris. She could not accept money for her guide services as it was against the law since she was uncertified. This woman was brilliant and knew an unbelievable amount of the history of practically every street and neighborhood in Paris and she was eager to share it. She truly was a marvel.

It was through Martine that I met a remarkable woman, Shahla, who was born in Iran, now officially a resident of New Zealand but beginning her own private tours for women in Italy (www.womentouritaly.com). She was a classy, intelligent woman who was easy to like.

All three of us sauntered through Montmarte one afternoon and rested on a bench near a tiny cemetery. There, on the next bench, was an interesting looking woman. I wanted a photo so I approached her in my fledgling French and asked if I could take a photo of her. Martine, translated happily from her bench. The lady was something out of a different time. I guessed her to be in her fifties. She wore a white, off-the shoulder blouse, a full, voluminous skirt, belt, netted stockings and a full array of jewelry but little make up. Her hair was in a bun and she looked like a former showgirl (Shahla told me later she thought she might have been a prostitute). She, amused at my interest, nodded her approval and we all began to talk together as I shot photo after photo. Apparently, she had been (years earlier) a dancer who danced for parties in "private salons". Wouldn't I have loved to interview her about her life! What stories she might have told me!

Shahla and I managed to plan to go to a famous "nightclub" in Montmartre after dinner in the area, "Lapin Agile", which had been painted by Picasso. The painting sold for over $50 million smackers in the eighties (what would it be worth now?) and the painting was now at the New York Metropolitan Museum of Art. The property looked quaint from the outside. So, having made earlier reservations, after dinner we strolled over. Montmartre was very beautiful at night with the basilica all lit up. We paid the admission fee and entered into the dim red, chintzy interior, slowly navigating our way to the hard wooden benches to sit. Along with admission one got their selection of a small, cheap red house wine, Cherry Brandy or water. Go crazy, girls!

Shahla asked me if I saw Jesus. Huh? "Well, I am a Christian but I haven't exactly *seen* him…" I answered, hesitant.

"No!" she laughed "over there"…. I looked to where her fingers pointed in the murky room and as my eyes adjusted I saw a huge, bigger-than-life statue of Jesus on the crucifix!

"Omigosh, he is watching us!" I exclaimed. "We can't get away from him, not even in Montmartre!" What an extraordinary thing to have in such a place.

The owners sang and played instruments and in general bored us to tears. We left after one hour thinking we had been there for three. It was one of the oddest French experiences I have had. Take my word for it, Picasso's painting might be worth seeing but this was not.

All these women added such dimension to my experience. Any would be welcomed in my home today and I was blessed our paths crossed.

Finally, as I approached my departure, I had been waiting all summer to see the ballet at Opera Garnier, the one I had stood so long in line for. "La Petite Danseuse De Degas" was spectacular. It filled the senses. To just sit in this opera house makes one feel like royalty; it is that exquisite. The Chagall ceiling mural dances his characters above the audiences tempting all to look up instead of at the stage. Each gorgeous seat is individually positioned and cushioned for an elegant guest, the closest I will ever to get sitting on a throne.

This ballet was the best I have ever seen in France. It was like watching a Degas painting or bronze sculpture come alive. And there I was in the 7th row centre seat. I re-live that evening over and over again in my memory. What a privilege. To say it was a WOW night and that my N.O. was off the charts is no exaggeration.

Strengthened, fortified fully, I was ready to return home, to life as it was, to my children and their crises, to my home and my friends. I was ready for anything.

As you can see my life had many dimensions…

Thirty One

So you ask: "Why Paris?"

There is a special place in the world for every heart that beats. A place we can go to and always feel happy. For some it may be Tuscany, others Melbourne, still others Mongolia. OK, Mongolia may be stretch; how about Santa Fe? *How about your home?* It really doesn't matter. What matters is that you recognize its blessings and gifts. For me, Paris was magic. I drenched myself in it all. It has always held that perfect allure. On all nine trips I never felt I had enough of it. I always felt blessed to be there. I always wanted to return. To say it was a kaleidoscope of colorful experiences is an understatement.

I wandered down those rues and boulevards like the twenty-one year old I once was, in awe of everything as I had been forty years earlier. I gallivanted around Versailles on foot and bike breathing in the magnificent formal gardens with their elaborate, ornate fountains and speculated who had walked where I was standing, who had frequented the forests where my bicycle took me: kings and queens!

I discovered museums that even my French friends didn't know existed. I attended lectures and art exhibits from old-world jewelry to Toulouse Lautrec posters to the exquisite Tiffany exhibit in Luxembourg Palais.

I met more international people in Paris than on the many continents I have traveled over a lifetime. I met, as I have told you the President of the Assembly Nationale, our equivalent of Congress, who was most cordial and charming. I got to know the local people of my neighborhoods: the baker (of course), the chocolatiers (you knew that), the seamstress, the hair stylist, the grocers and my favorite "farmers" at the open air markets, which were in every arrondissement *by law*! Through my hiking group I was befriended by wonderfully warm French friends who marched through rues and forests with me. When I met a man from "Georgia", I knew from his look, accent and dress he was from the former Soviet Union not one of the thirteen original colonies.

For someone who is into history, music, art and architecture, Paris is nirvana. Endless concerts in historic cathedrals and chateaus, constantly changing exhibits, ballet, opera; they defined Paris and settled like a treasure in my heart. It was a fragrant ointment that washed over the wounds of my spirit and healed my soul.

One gothic Cathedral after another enthralled me. There was more stained glass than I could fathom. I became my own expert on Monet. I learned who gave free and low cost tours and concerts. The many metro musicians and street entertainers dared me to live in the moment, lured me to enjoy "the now". And I did! Eckhart Tolle would be proud!

In other words, although I have shared some funny scenarios about the men in my life, they actually had little to do with any reason I was in Paris. Yes, yes, they added to the sensory dimension of it all, *no doubt about that!* Sigh. When I stepped off that plane *I had no idea my joy would be magnified on so many levels.* But the lack of a partners or companions should never stop anyone from enjoying their life fully. Even Anne Morrow Lindberg in her "Gift From the Sea" agreed: "If it is a woman's function to give, she must be replenished too."

Adventure is not going to knock on my door but I can knock on the door of adventure! I went to Paris for me. I had to leave my reality to find myself. I put everyone else's problems to the wayside and concentrated unabashedly on moi. Perhaps, you can do that from your back porch or with a new career, hobby or a get-away weekend. You may find your Paris within (it costs much less, too!).

For me, living out a dream brought my endorphins back into order. It gave me back my balance. With that balance happiness, even joy resurfaced. Happiness must not weigh on who loves you (or who doesn't); it is not a person or a destination. *It lies within* wherever you are. Attitude is everything, isn't it? Did you ever notice that with an improved attitude *everything* improves? Gratitude enhances the chances of being more available, more present to receive the happiness, the beauty that surrounds all of us daily. I never felt I was chasing happiness; I was chasing *balance* to the challenges in my life. Once I found the balance, happiness was waiting. Unhealthy self-sacrifice won't make me a saint because the cost of self-neglect is a loss to me and the people in my world.

No one on earth has it all. We all face demons; we survive heartache, loneliness, failures, disappearing portfolios and betrayal. Those things may not change. None of us can actually run away from home and our problems for long, can we? Whatever direction we take they resurface. Those challenges will follow wherever we venture. Sometimes there are just no easy answers. Joy mixes with sorrow; both make us what we are today and what we will be tomorrow. *Adversity strengthens but it strengthens us if we come from a position of balance. Otherwise, it buries us.*

If I have my balance the *impact* of my issues, the crises in my life may be minimized because now I approach them from a different, *stronger* place. I am better able to deal with them because of this newfound balance. I took what I needed. For me, it could not have come in an overnight. I also have learned that I can loose that precious balance if I overdo something like I had been in the springtime with too many Jean Pierres.

My son, the light of my life, announced recently he is returning to the hospital to see if he might now, with new surgical options, be a candidate for a second brain surgery. As always he remains uncomplaining. He is filled with optimism and hope and *if he can be, I must be.*

I want to make one thing clear: Brian has taught me how to love, fully and selflessly. His adversity has helped me to grow not just as a mother but also as a human being. He has never been a burden; he has always been a privilege. I would not be the human being I am today had I not the opportunity to grow through his affliction. The late Christopher Reeve once said: "Once you choose hope, anything's possible." Brian lives that. What an inspiration he is to me!

As a middle-aged woman I had been up and down and all around with such a variety of excuses for not being happy it would amaze you. Oscar Wilde wrote "What seems to us as bitter trials are often blessings in disguise". I have found out that I can be in pain, hurting, heartsick and still experience happiness.

A few years ago I learned a valuable lesson. We had enormous fires in southern California. Properties burned to the ground, people were caught in horrific scenes and injuries and death reports infused our daily news. At the time, I was suffering from a painful shoulder condition waiting for Miser Permanente to do surgery on me. After the fires were over I stumbled into a person who worked on my street for our HOA maintenance organization. While he and his family escaped, they lost everything in the fire. Spontaneously, I offered to help him.

I sent letters to all my neighbors, to my friends, to my Church asking for help for this family. I got my women's group to sponsor them, as well. Then, I sat back and watched a small miracle happen. One at a time, people began bringing food, clothing, furniture even a new refrigerator. Checks and gift certificates arrived in the mail totaling thousands of dollars. My women's group supplied everything anyone could ever need for their kitchen. I threw a reception for the family at Christmas and invited everyone who had contributed to this family's welfare. It was truly one of the happiest holiday seasons I have ever had, and the pain, for that eight-week period, subsided entirely.

Oh, yes, I knew it was there but *my happiness outweighed it*. Now, for me, that was a lesson to be learned. You can be in physical or emotional pain and still accept happiness. What a wonderful thing to embrace!

Women survive so much: cramps, birth, menopause, disappointing husbands, insincere lovers, divorces, down-sizing, diagnoses, death of friends, aging bodies and disillusionment, some of them *simultaneously*. It is called *life!* We survive life usually with courage, often with dignity. Still, the expectation is for us to be superwomen; that can be exhausting and impossible. We give endlessly to our families, our places of worship, our communities, and our world. We wear the red badge of courage and proudly proclaim ourselves "survivors". Then we forget to balance those responsibilities with some of the very pleasures that once gave us joy.

Let's rethink that, shall we? In the midst of these never-ending challenges of our lives, we can no longer consider ourselves survivors; we *must* be *thrivers*!

It is *mandatory to thriving that we give in that same, dedicated way to ourselves* as we have given to our world. OK, so maybe it can't happen every day, but it *must* happen *regularly* if we are to be more than survivors. It *must* happen if we are to be fully evolved human beings. It *must* happen if we are to live the rich, multi-dimensional lives we were destined to live. Finally, it *must* happen if we are to regain and retain our *balance*.

I renewed my connection with the world. I am living fully as I was meant to. I honored myself and the value of my life and because of that I have built my capacity for helping others in the future. I have returned home from my escapades a stronger, better version of myself. I have said adieu to my old friend, Prozac and am happier in my every day, even if I don't have a cute Frenchman knocking on my door on New Year's Eve! *His loss*!

My joie de vivre has returned! I once again am embracing life!

I read a wonderful quote recently, author unknown:

"One day at a time—this is enough. Do not look back and grieve over the past for it is gone; and do not be troubled about the future, for it has not yet come. Live in the present, and make it so beautiful it will be worth remembering."

That is what I am doing. I am appreciating the moment, living fully in its beauty. You see, I am – most definitely – *not* just a survivor. *I am a thriver*!

Made in the USA
Charleston, SC
11 August 2012